SET AN EXAMPLE

How to Lead Others & Live Out
God's Presence in the World

Syeeda J. Echols

WWW.TRUEVINEPUBLISHING.ORG

Set an Example
Syeeda J. Echols

Published by
True Vine Publishing Co.
810 Dominican Dr.
Nashville, TN 37228
www.TrueVinePublishing.org

Printed in the United States of America—First printing.

This book is dedicated to

my grandmother, Inez

my mother, Evelyn

my sister, Aisha

TABLE OF CONTENTS

INTRODUCTION

"Arise, shine; for your light has come, and the glory of the
Lord has risen upon you."
- Isaiah 60:1 NRSV

What if leadership is not about power, but presence? What if it is not about position, but the posture of your heart?

We often picture leadership as a title, a platform, or a stage. But leadership in the Kingdom of God is deeper than influence. It is the courage to live differently and love intentionally, even when it is not popular.

You may not have a title. You may not feel ready. But if God has placed something on your heart, that is a calling. If others watch how you live and listen when you speak, you are already leading.

Before we dive into how you can walk this out, let me tell you a bit about my own leadership journey and the lessons God taught me along the way.

In 2015, I was living in Guatemala and teaching second grade at an international school. I had been in education for several years when a new position opened; one that would place me in a leadership role training about fifty educators and paraeducators serving more than five hundred children in kindergarten through fifth grade.

It was not just a promotion; it was a calling. I did not see it that way. When they offered me the job, I froze. I had not attended leadership training. I did not have a degree in leadership. All I could see was what I lacked. So I turned it down, packed up my apartment, left the country, and moved back to the United States.

The truth is, I ran.

I let fear and doubt speak louder than God's voice. I thought leadership required more than what I had. What I did not understand was that God does not call the ready. He calls the willing. I did not need to run. I needed to trust that God would walk with me through it.

After I left, I prayed a simple, honest prayer: "God, I do not see leadership in myself, but I want You to form it in me. Train me to lead. Teach me to see myself the way You do."

He did. Leaving Guatemala marked the beginning of my journey into leadership. What followed were years of being stretched, shaped, challenged, and prepared. I did not receive a title right away. What I received instead was formation through hardship, through opportunities I did not feel qualified for, and through mentors who saw more in me than I saw in myself.

During that season, God drew me closer to Him as began studying young and unexpected leaders throughout Scripture.

I spent time with the stories of Joshua, the daughters of Zelophehad, Judges, Ruth, Esther, Huldah the prophetess, King David, Elisha, the Minor Prophets, the disciples in Acts, Paul, and Timothy. For years, I returned to their lives, paying close attention to how God raised them up and how leadership was modeled, formed, and passed from one generation to the next.

That is when I came across Paul's commission to Timothy, a promising young leader who was mentored and encouraged to walk boldly in his purpose. Paul's words to Timothy are deeply inspiring and offer a standard that I believe every Christian leader can live by, especially 1 Timothy 4:12: *"Let no one despise your youth, but set the believers an example in speech and conduct, in love, in faith, and in purity."*

God gave me this verse and imprinted it on my heart. At the time, I had no idea He would lead me to live it out and then make it the heartbeat of this book. That is exactly what He did. First Timothy 4:12 became more than a memory verse. It became a call to action, a standard to pursue, and a framework for formation.

Now that you know how this book came to be, let us talk about why God called me to write it and you to read it.

God wants you to know you were created for more. The Lord is raising up a generation of leaders who follow Him and think with a Kingdom mindset. We are the next generation of leaders. We are being prepared to step into roles as others transition out. Yet many of us do not feel ready. Sometimes that hesitation comes from a lack of training. Other times, it is the fear of carrying the weight of responsibility. If that is you, you are not alone.

Fear, doubt, and insecurity often appear in the lives of those called to do great things. We must use spiritual weapons to combat those thoughts. While your feelings are real, fear and doubt do not come from God. He would never call you to greatness and then paralyze you with fear.

Ask yourself: who would want to keep you from shining your light, revealing God's glory, and making Him known to the nations? Exactly. That is the enemy's tactic.

As you read this book, you may experience both joy and doubt. The joy comes from God. He is present and wants you to do His will. The doubt comes from the enemy, who does not want you to do anything good for God.

My prayer is that you will accept this invitation, because you are needed. I will not pretend it is glamorous.

The Bible warned that in the last days people would become lovers of self, prefer lies over truth, and seek teachers who only tell them what they want to hear (see 2 Timothy 3:1–5; 4:3–4). Politics, churches, education, media, and families are affected.

Politicians manipulate truth for power and profit. Some judges and lawyers pervert justice for the sake of prestige or financial gain. Religious leaders sometimes preach prosperity over purpose. Many seek God primarily for personal benefit rather than to fulfill the purpose for which they were created, which is to glorify God and make disciples.

Educators are pressured to uphold systems of power and privilege. Social media, which could connect us, often divides through misinformation, hatred, and false identities. Perhaps most heartbreaking of all, the family is under attack. Infidelity is marketed as entertainment. Divorce rates are rising. In some homes, deep division has led to harm between parents and children. Fewer families are gathering to read the Word, to pray, or to seek God's wisdom as a household. Instead of leaning into what God actually says, many reshape Scripture to suit personal preferences or justify behavior. When godly leadership is missing in the home, it becomes harder to pass down truth, character, and spiritual legacy to the next generation.

This is why Moses urged the Israelites to keep God's Word close, not only in their hearts, but also in their homes. *"He commanded them to teach these truths diligently to their children and to talk about them throughout daily life. They were to write God's commands on their doorposts, on their hands, and on their foreheads"* (Deuteronomy 6:6–9). When God's Word is not taught, lived, and remembered regularly we lose sight of who He is, who we are, and the purpose we were created to fulfill.

Many today are growing up unaware of God's character, their identity, and the authority they carry to bring change. The farther we drift from God's Word, the more disconnected we become from our identity and purpose. That is why you are here. You are the leader we need for the future. God is calling you to be more and to do more than you imagined. As we examine 1 Timothy 4:12, I pray that you will accept the call to lead others to Jesus.

Paul's letters to Timothy reveal the heart of a leader who exhorted him to remain faithful, grounded, and steadfast in his calling. He taught Timothy to set a godly example, knowing the world needed righteous leadership. This book is not just about visibility or growth. *Set an Example* shifts the lens to the internal life of the leader and how that life shapes others. It is not about climbing higher but about becoming whole, faithful, and grounded in Christ.

Christian leadership does not begin on a stage or in a corner office. It comes from the intimacy of knowing Christ so deeply that His life becomes visible through yours. It is not about leading more people but about leading from a place of surrender, where your example becomes the message.

Paul's commission to Timothy was never about being impressive, important, or elevated in the eyes of others. Paul's leadership stood in stark contrast to the Pharisees, who sought status, attention, and external displays of holiness while neglecting the heart of God. Timothy was called to live differently, to lead with grace, integrity, and the power of the Holy Spirit. That same call still stands.

In a world desperate for compassionate speech, consistent character, and genuine love, God is raising up leaders not to perform but to embody His presence. Just as Paul traveled and sent Timothy to strengthen communities of faith, God is still sending us to bring light into dark places. Through this book, we will explore what it means to lead with character shaped by Scripture and a life guided by the Spirit, so that God's love may permeate our world, not through outward display or empty religion, but through how we treat one another and how we show up.

If we are to reflect His presence in the world, we must return to His Word. Together, we will study Scripture and align our lives with it, learning from the same charge Paul gave to Timothy, to set an example in speech, in conduct, in love, in faith, and in purity.

At the end of each chapter, you will find:
- A closing prayer
- Scriptures to memorize
- Personal reflection questions

At the back of the book, you will find:
- A small group discussion guide designed to help you walk through these lessons with others who are also growing in faith and leadership
- Space to record insights and group takeaways

This is your leadership guide to live out the call God has placed on your life. You do not have to run or remain stuck. This book is here to help you accept your assignment from God and live it out fully.

Just as when Paul first wrote to Timothy, the world around us is brimming with confusion, compromise, and competing "truths." Timothy was sent to confront false teaching and strengthen a weary church. His leadership was not optional; it was urgent. So is yours.

Take heart. You carry something holy, God's presence within you. The same Spirit who empowered Timothy to teach truth, correct error, and lead with courage will guide you. He equips you with wisdom, steadies you with peace, and ignites you with boldness. The Spirit of God will be your strength and power sending you into the world with purpose and courage, not in your own strength, but in His.

Are you ready? Your leadership starts now.

CHAPTER 1

DO NOT LET ANYONE LOOK DOWN ON YOU BECAUSE YOU ARE YOUNG

"I praise You, for I am fearfully and wonderfully made.
Wonderful are Your works; that I know very well."
— Psalm 139:14

God is the giver of gifts. With divine wisdom, He chooses leaders not according to human standards but for His own purpose and glory. We do not pick our abilities or calling; we are simply born with them. As Scripture reminds us, *"we are what He has made us, created in Christ Jesus for good works, which God prepared beforehand to be our way of life"* (Ephesians 2:10).

For too long, society has pushed certain images of leadership: tall, older, and male. But God does not measure leaders by appearance. He searches the heart and calls forth what He has already placed within.

This truth is woven throughout the Bible in the stories of the many leaders God chose to carry out His will.

What If Everything You Believed About Leadership Was Too Small?

Many of us have absorbed a narrow idea of what a leader looks like: loud, older, extroverted, polished. We think we have to be more qualified, more experienced, more liked. But God's definition of leadership is not rooted in popularity or perfection. It is rooted in obedience.

If you believe leadership is only for a certain type of person, you may miss how God is already calling you to lead right where you are.

Biblical Leadership Was Never About Perfection

Nearly every major biblical leader began their journey with some form of self-doubt. Moses, when confronted with his call to lead the Israelites out of Egypt, responded with uncertainty, asking, "Who am I that I should go to Pharaoh?" His insecurity about his identity and speech revealed just how inadequate he felt.

Similarly, Sarah laughed when God told her she would bear a child in old age. Her laughter was not joy at first, but disbelief. She could not see how the promise could come to pass through someone like her. Gideon, hiding in a winepress when the angel of the Lord found him, said, "My clan is the weakest… and I am the least." His words revealed a man who did not see his own potential.

Jeremiah, too, was overwhelmed by the weight of his call, responding, "I am only a youth," as if his age disqualified him from carrying God's message. Even Mary, the young virgin chosen to bear the Savior of the world, asked the angel, "How can this be?" not out of rebellion, but from a place of honest wonder and uncertainty.

What is remarkable is that God did not rebuke any of them for their questions. He did not turn away from their fears or frustrations. Instead, He met their doubt with reassurance. He affirmed their identity, reminded them of His presence, and promised to be with them every step of the way. Leadership in Scripture was never about being fully prepared or self-confident. It was always about being willing and available. God's pattern is clear: He chooses leaders not based on readiness, but on His redemptive purpose, and then shapes them through His Spirit.

When we examine the lives of those God used, we see a theme of unexpected leadership. Rahab, a foreigner and a prostitute, made a bold confession of faith and helped Israel spy out the land. She became part of the lineage of Jesus. Jael, a homemaker, delivered Israel by taking down an enemy general with nothing more than a tent peg and courage.

Nehemiah, a cupbearer with no military experience, led the rebuilding of Jerusalem's walls through vision, prayer, and persistence. Esther, a young orphan raised by her cousin, became queen and risked her life to save her people from genocide. Her bravery changed the course of a nation.

David, the youngest and most overlooked among his brothers, was anointed king while still tending sheep. His rise to leadership reminds us that God sees what others dismiss. Timothy, a young man raised in the faith by his mother and grandmother, was entrusted by Paul to lead churches despite his youth. Paul himself, once a persecutor of Christians, became one of the most powerful voices of the early Church after encountering Christ. His story proves that even our worst mistakes do not disqualify us when God calls our name.

Every excuse we can offer, whether it is our age, our past, our background, or our weaknesses, has already been spoken by someone else in Scripture. In each case, God responded not with rejection, but with invitation. He does not look for perfection. He looks for availability, humility, and trust. If He could use a stammering shepherd, a barren woman, a fearful warrior, and a teenage girl, He can use you.

Even Paul, a man of deep faith and wide influence, appointed capable leaders regardless of gender or background (Romans 16). He believed in equipping others to carry the gospel as he moved from place to place sharing the Good News. The early church was filled with individuals who did not "fit the mold," but their faith made them fit for service.

This same invitation still stands. It is not reserved for those with titles or platforms. It is for anyone willing to say yes to God's call. I know this because I have lived it.

My First Sermon

Reflecting on my own journey, I recall a pivotal moment during my time in seminary. It was my first semester, and a church invited me to preach. The idea of preaching terrified me. So I signed up for a student preaching symposium to get practice. I had heard the audience would be small, and a panel of professors and local pastors would offer feedback. As someone who thrives on coaching and appreciates both encouragement and constructive criticism, it seemed like the perfect opportunity to practice before doing the real thing on Sunday morning.

On the day of the sermon, fear hit me like a wave. My chest tightened. My mind began to swirl with doubt.

Moments before it was my turn to preach, I burst into tears. Panic attacks have come and gone throughout my life, and in that moment, it felt like every internalized doubt came rushing to the surface. The tears came unexpectedly. I stepped into the hallway, hands trembling, eyes welling up, struggling to breathe.

A friend noticed me and quickly wrapped me in a hug. She knew I was nervous, so she sat with me. "You are here because God placed you here," she whispered. "You have done the work. You have prayed. You have studied. You can do this."

Then, as if sent on divine assignment, one of the panel judges happened to walk by. He saw my face in my hands and paused. He called my name, and when I looked up, he saw my red eyes.

"I saw you earlier," he said softly. "You walked in with such confidence. What has changed?"

"I do not know if I can do this," I admitted, embarrassed, barely able to speak.

Through tears, I told him about my fears: how I had never preached before, how the room was full of veteran preachers, and how I was afraid they would think I did not belong behind the pulpit. He looked at me with deep conviction. "Listen, you are not alone. You are not here to impress anyone. You are here to deliver a message that God placed inside you. We are excited to hear it. Go in there and give what He gave you." Then he prayed and allowed me to take a moment to gather myself.

His prayer steadied me. I returned to the room, heart still racing but steadier. I stood behind the pulpit, hands damp and eyes scanning the room. I delivered the message I had poured over for weeks. I had practiced every line, but nerves compressed what should have been a twenty-minute message into just eight minutes. Like a plane that lifts off too soon and lands too fast, my first sermon was over before I knew it.

Then came the feedback. One panelist leaned forward and said, "Your storytelling was magnetic. You brought us in from the very first line."

Another pastor added, "Your closing, walking through the names from Scripture, was so powerful, I am borrowing that in my own sermons."

One remarked, "The way you wove Scripture through the message is a skill many seasoned preachers still do not have. Do not lose that."

Then one said something I will never forget: "You reminded me of Walter Brueggemann."

To my surprise, the tears returned. This time, they were not from fear. They came from relief, from gratitude, and from the overwhelming kindness these seasoned pastors had shown to someone just starting out. Their encouragement broke something open in me. They also offered tips for improvement, one of which was to preach with confidence and accept the mantle God had given me.

I thanked them and stepped down from the pulpit to return to my seat. Something had shifted inside me. I did not realize it then, but that moment marked the beginning of something I never expected. I did not walk away with a polished sermon or a perfect performance. I walked away with something better: a sense of calling. Their words helped silence the voice of fear I had carried for far too long. For the first time, I began to believe that maybe God really could use me. Not someday when I felt more ready, but right then, just as I was.

Since that day in 2017, I have preached across the country, in hospitals, churches of various denominations, and in chapels on college campuses. That feeling of doubt still tries to visit, but it does not get the final say. I have learned to fight those thoughts by studying Scripture and standing firm in who God says I am, and by remembering how I have seen Him move in my life again and again.

Looking back, I now realize that the strength to stand behind a pulpit did not begin in that room. It was built long before, in the quiet spaces where God was shaping my character through faith and obedience. My story was not an exception. It is part of a pattern God has always used to prepare leaders long before anyone else sees them.

The Quiet Work of Preparation

Leadership does not begin with a microphone. It begins with obedience. It does not start on a platform in front of crowds; it starts in quiet spaces where no one is watching. Before God entrusts someone with public influence, He often tests their private faithfulness. We see this pattern throughout Scripture, where some of the most impactful leaders were first proven in humble, hidden places.

Before David wore a crown and led a nation, he played a harp in the presence of a tormented king. Long before anyone recognized him as a warrior or ruler, David was tending sheep, writing psalms, and serving Saul in obscurity. His worship in private prepared him for warfare in public. His obedience with a harp made him trustworthy with a sword. God developed David's character in solitude before revealing his calling in the spotlight.

Before Elisha ever spoke as a prophet, he faithfully served Elijah. For years, he was known as "the one who poured water on the hands of Elijah" (2 Kings 3:11). He watched, learned, and waited. He was not chasing a title; he was seeking God's presence. When the time came for Elijah to be taken up to heaven, Elisha was ready. His years of humble service became the foundation for his double-portion anointing.

Before Joshua became Israel's leader, he spent decades watching Moses. He lingered near the tent of meeting, where God spoke with Moses face-to-face. He observed how Moses handled crises, how he interceded for the people, and how he listened to God. Joshua's leadership was not built on ambition but on apprenticeship. His readiness came from proximity to a leader who walked with God.

Before Timothy pastored churches and preached with boldness, he sat at Paul's feet. He received letters filled with instruction, correction, and encouragement. Timothy was teachable. He did not rush the process or demand his own platform. He allowed God to shape him through mentorship and relationship. His leadership was not birthed in isolation, but in community and submission to godly guidance.

Sometimes we are afraid to lead. Other times, the call of God stirs something so deep in us that we are ready to run full speed ahead. We want to say yes, take the mic, step into the spotlight. We are eager to make an impact. In our excitement, we can forget that calling does not always mean an immediate platform. God still does His deepest work in hidden places. He develops character before He gives visibility. He builds endurance before influence.

We often want the opportunity without the preparation. God trains us in the quiet places. Those hidden seasons are where we learn to serve, to listen, and to trust Him long before anyone else sees it. Those unseen seasons are sacred. They are where your faith is stretched, your character is shaped, and your trust is tested. Do not despise the days when no one sees you. Those are the days God is planting roots that will sustain you later. You do not have to wait to be seen to be sent. If God has called you, He has already equipped you. The same Spirit who raised Jesus from the dead is living and active within you, and that changes everything.

What You Carry Is Divine

In John 14:16–17, Jesus promises, *"And I will ask the Father, and He will give you another Advocate to be with you forever. This is the Spirit of truth… you know Him, because He abides with you, and He will be in you."* That promise was not just for the disciples. It is for all of us. As a believer, you carry the Holy Spirit. The same Spirit who empowered Jesus' ministry and raised Him from the grave now lives within you. That is not only a spiritual comfort; it is a divine commissioning.

It is normal to feel insecure. We question our appearance, our speech, our background, our relationships. God already accounted for all of that when He called you. He knew your personality, your habits, your fears, your past, and your doubts. He still chose you.

Paul's words to Timothy still ring true today: *"Do not let anyone look down on you because you are young"* (1 Timothy 4:12). He was not just encouraging Timothy; he was commissioning him. Timothy had the gifting. Paul saw it. More importantly, God had placed it there, and Paul wanted him to walk confidently in the power of the Spirit.

You, too, carry that same Spirit. Walk boldly, not because of your own ability, but because of the Spirit within you.

Let Your Life Speak

The best way to overcome doubt is not by striving harder, but by living with consistent, godly character. Leadership is not about proving your worth. It is about reflecting God's character. When you live with integrity, your life becomes the message. When people see God's hand on your life, it can awaken faith in their own. Your courage reminds them they are not too young, too broken, or too late. Your obedience gives them permission to obey.

So do not let anyone look down on you because you are young. More importantly, do not look down on yourself. The same Spirit who raised Jesus from the dead lives in you. That truth alone changes everything. You were not just saved. You were sent. Your life is not random. Your leadership matters.

You do not have to have it all together. Be faithful with what is in your hands. Where God has placed you is where your leadership begins. When you lead with character that reflects Christ, your life becomes the evidence that He is real, present, and still calling people today.

In the chapters ahead, we will look closely at the charge Paul gave to Timothy and how it still calls us today. Together, we will walk through what that looks like: how to lead with your words, your actions, your love, your faith, and your purity.

Scriptures for the Journey

Take time this week to read these verses slowly. Choose one to memorize, meditate on, or write in your journal as a reminder of who God has called you to be.

Have I not commanded you? Be strong and courageous. Do not be afraid; do not be discouraged, for the Lord your God will be with you wherever you go. — Joshua 1:9 NIV; see also Deuteronomy 31:6 NIV

But the Lord said to Samuel, "Do not consider his appearance or his height, for I have rejected him. The Lord does not look at the things people look at. People look at the outward appearance, but the Lord looks at the heart." — 1 Samuel 16:7 NIV

I praise you because I am fearfully and wonderfully made; your works are wonderful, I know that full well. — Psalm 139:14 NIV

"Alas, Sovereign Lord," I said, "I do not know how to speak; I am too young." But the Lord said to me, "Do not say, 'I am too young.' You must go to everyone I send you to and say whatever I command you." — Jeremiah 1:6–7 NIV

For it is God who works in you to will and to act in order to fulfill his good purpose. — Philippians 2:13 NIV

Pause + Reflect

Use these questions to gently explore what stood out to you in this chapter. There is no pressure to have perfect answers. Just space to process, pray, and grow.

1. When you think about leadership, do you see yourself as someone God could use? Why or why not?

2. What gift or strength have you been hesitant to use, and what might be holding you back?

3. How can you show leadership this week with your friends, family, campus, or work?

Prayer

Father,

Thank You for calling me even when I felt unprepared. Help me trust Your purpose, steady me in fear, and remind me I am chosen and created for good works. Make me a light for others, and let my faith, love, and confidence reflect You. Strengthen me to follow Your calling and hear Your voice more than any other's.

In Jesus' name,
Amen.

CHAPTER 2

SET AN EXAMPLE IN SPEECH

*"Do not let any unwholesome talk come out of your mouths,
but only what is helpful for building others up according to
their needs, that it may benefit those who listen."*
— Ephesians 4:29 NIV

Words Are Never Just Words
They build, they break, they bless, they burn.
As a leader, your words will become one of your most powerful
tools. Your speech can open doors or close them, heal hearts or
harden them, elevate people or crush their confidence without
even raising your voice.

We often emphasize productivity in leadership: deadlines
met, tasks completed, goals achieved. Yet God examines more
than our output. He looks at how we communicate, how we
instruct, how we correct, and how we affirm. He listens to not
only what we say, but how we say it.

One of the most essential traits of a godly leader is the ability to steward speech well. You could have the most strategic mind in the room, but if your words are reckless, sarcastic, impatient, or harsh, your influence will suffer. It is entirely possible to speak truth and still do harm.

When You Are "Right" but Still Wrong

Have you ever walked away from a conversation knowing you were right but still feeling convicted about how you handled it? That feeling does not come from being wrong about the facts. It comes from knowing that your delivery lacked compassion. The issue was not your point; it was your posture. Truth, when served without grace, can cut deeply. It is possible to win an argument and lose a relationship in the process. It is possible to silence someone with facts while simultaneously breaking their spirit.

Some of my deepest regrets in leadership and communication do not come from what I said, but how I said it. I have delivered statements that were correct but laced with sarcasm, impatience, or pride. I have spoken quickly, harshly, or dismissively, and later had to return to those moments with an apology. Not because I was wrong in content, but because I failed in compassion. The truth was right, yet my tone was wrong.

There is a subtle but significant difference between speaking boldly and speaking harshly. As leaders, we are called to deliver truth in love. That means not only what we say, but how we say it should reflect the heart of Christ. Even correction can be life-giving when delivered with humility and grace. A harsh tone may secure temporary compliance; a gracious tone fosters lasting transformation.

In leadership, tone is everything. The way we say something can invite others into growth or push them into silence. It can open the door for healing or shut it tight with shame. The goal is not merely to be heard; it is to be understood, respected, and trusted. That starts with recognizing that every word carries weight and every tone sets the atmosphere. Choose both wisely.

Words That Left a Mark

Growing up, I can recall the exact words that shaped me, for better or worse. Words like "God is going to do something great through you" lit something inside me. Words like "You're too much" or "You talk too much" made me want to shrink. The words we carry, especially those spoken in our formative years, become internal scripts. They play on repeat unless replaced by truth.

I have seen adults paralyzed in their purpose because of something a parent, teacher, or coach said decades ago. A single sentence spoken without care can chain someone for years. Nevertheless, here is the hope: a single sentence, spoken with intention and love, can break that chain just as fast.

You have that power to speak life over dry bones, to move a mountain into the sea, and to make the sun stand still. However, to be a good speaker you must be an even better listener.

Listening Is Leading

When I accepted my first leadership role, I assumed I had to talk a lot: cast vision, give instructions, offer insight. A mentor said something that flipped my approach: "Spend your first month listening."

So that is what I did. I scheduled one-on-one meetings. I asked team members to tell me about their dreams, their frustrations, and their favorite parts of the job. I listened without interrupting or fixing. I asked follow-up questions. I took notes. By the time I spoke publicly, people were more inclined to listen because I had listened first. I learned the culture, the spoken and unspoken norms. I knew who spoke up in meetings and who collaborated behind closed doors.

Leadership is not only about having a voice; it is about recognizing the voices with power around you.

Heaven's Plumb Line for My Words

James 3 is the plumb line I hold against my words, revealing whether they align with Heaven or drift toward harm. Every day, I fall short. This chapter does not coddle; it convicts. It shows me what I sound like not only to people, but to heaven. It exposes how quickly my tongue can drift from blessing to backlash, from building to burning. Yet it also reveals the hope that I am not left to tame it alone. The same Spirit who once placed a burning coal on the prophet's lips now lets Heaven's fire purify mine.

James 3:6 says, *"The tongue is a fire, a world of evil among the parts of the body."* That is not poetic exaggeration. That is divine warning. Scripture does not soften the truth about our speech. It calls it what it is: powerful, dangerous, and capable of devastation. Left unchecked, the tongue does not merely reflect sin; it multiplies it.

James compares our words to a single spark that can set an entire forest ablaze. One careless comment in a meeting can shift the entire atmosphere. One sarcastic jab can make someone question whether they belong. One text message, stripped of tone and wrapped in assumption, can dismantle a relationship that took years to build. One joke meant to be harmless can plant seeds of shame that grow into silent wounds.

Even the words we "do not mean" have consequences. Sarcasm may sound clever, yet it often conceals cruelty. Passive-aggression can masquerade as politeness but it poisons trust. Gossip cloaked in prayer requests still stirs division. The tongue does not need volume to be violent. Even whispered words can wound.

This is why our words must be surrendered to the Spirit. Every conversation, every comment, and every caption either invites the Kingdom or echoes the enemy. The Holy Spirit is not only present in our preaching or in our worship. He is present or grieved in our speech. What we say matters. How we say it matters. Whether we speak in love or in bitterness, in healing or in pride, it all reveals what is happening in the heart.

James is not only warning us. He is discipling us. He is calling us into maturity that refuses to separate speech from sanctification. Our mouths are not neutral. They are altars. The fire that rests on them should be holy.

So treat your words accordingly. Speak with reverence. Repent when needed. Let your mouth become a vessel of grace, not a weapon of destruction. When the Holy Spirit fills your voice, He does not merely cleanse what you say; He changes the world through it.

The Ministry of Encouragement

Not everyone is called to preach from a pulpit. Everyone is called to minister with their mouth. Whether you are leading a team, parenting children, mentoring a friend, or interacting with strangers, your words carry the power to reflect God's love and truth.

You do not need a corner office to make a difference. A timely word such as "You're doing a great job," "You are growing," or "I see God in you" can shift someone's entire perspective. Simple affirmations can breathe life into weary souls and provide encouragement in moments when it is needed most.

Hebrews 3:13 says, *"Encourage one another daily."* Not occasionally; daily. Encouragement is not meant to be a rare occurrence or an empty gesture. It is meant to be a regular rhythm in our relationships, a spiritual discipline that strengthens community and fosters growth.

Throughout the New Testament, we are commanded to: *"Therefore encourage one another and build up each other, as indeed you are doing."*

— 1 Thessalonians 5:11 (NRSV)

"Don't grumble against one another, brothers and sisters, or you will be judged. The Judge is standing at the door!"

— James 5:9 (NIV)

"And let us consider how to provoke one another to love and good deeds"

— Hebrews 10:24 (NRSV)

These one-another commands are not optional; they are essential to the life of the Church. They remind us that encouragement is not flattery. This is ministry. It is how we lift each other, sharpen each other, and remind each other of who we are in Christ.

If you see something good in someone, say it. If you notice progress or maturity, acknowledge it. If you are proud of someone, let them know. You never know what private battle your words may be interrupting or what healing they might bring.

Stop Cursing What God Is Blessing

We must be careful not to speak against what God is blessing. It is easy to fall into the trap of critique, especially when something does not look the way we expect. Sometimes our negative words stem not from discernment but from jealousy. Instead of celebrating the growth or impact of others, we nitpick imperfections. We become quick to highlight flaws while overlooking the fruit of their labor. When God's hand is clearly on something, our opinions must take a back seat to His work.

There is a danger in judging based on surface-level discomfort. We may criticize a ministry's style, question someone's calling, or mock a movement simply because it does not align with our preferences. Jesus faced this. He healed on the Sabbath and was condemned for breaking tradition. He ate with sinners and was accused of compromising holiness. He was embodying the heart of God. His actions revealed the deeper purpose behind the law: love, mercy, and transformation.

If we are not vigilant, we will develop the same spirit as the Pharisees. We will become so concerned with appearances that we miss the miracles happening in front of us. The Pharisees were devoted and disciplined scholars, yet pride blinded them to the presence of the Messiah. We risk doing the same when we fixate on form rather than fruit, when we silence what we do not understand instead of seeking God's heart in it.

If God is blessing something, if lives are being changed, healing is taking place, and the gospel is going forth, then we need to be quiet or join in. There is no room in the Kingdom for self-righteous sabotage. Our role is not to critique every container God uses, but to honor the content He pours out. Let us be people who bless what God is blessing, who celebrate His move, and who have the humility to support what we may not fully understand.

Words in Conflict

It is not wrong to experience conflict. Conflict is often the doorway to growth, clarification, and deeper connection.

It becomes harmful when we weaponize our words. When conflict stops being about understanding and starts being about winning, words are no longer tools for truth, they become instruments of harm.

Paul's instruction in Ephesians 4:15 is clear: *"Speak the truth in love."* That pairing is essential. Love is the cushion; truth is the content. We need both. Truth without love is harsh. Love without truth is hollow. Together, they create space for honest, redemptive dialogue. A loving tone makes hard truths easier to hear and more likely to lead to transformation.

One practical way to approach difficult conversations is to use "I" statements. This focuses the conversation on how behavior impacted you rather than launching accusations. For instance, instead of saying, "You're always disrespectful," try saying, "I felt hurt by what was said earlier." Shifting the tone from blame to vulnerability creates a safer space for the other person to respond with humility rather than defensiveness.

It is also wise to delay tense conversations until emotions have settled. Proverbs 29:11 says, *"Fools give full vent to their rage, but the wise bring calm in the end."* Sometimes, wisdom means waiting. A wise leader understands that timing is everything. Even the right words, spoken at the wrong time, can do damage. Pray, pause, and let peace lead your approach.

As leaders, you will often need to facilitate mediation, whether among your children, employees, friends, or relatives. Your ability to lead well and listen well helps keep toxicity out of the workplace and prevents harmful words from unraveling your home.

Conduct That Corrects in Love

True leadership does not shy away from accountability. It welcomes it. We live in a culture that either cancels people without grace or excuses sin in the name of "minding our business." Neither cancel culture nor silence reflects the heart of Christ. God calls us to something better: to correct in love, restore in truth, and lead one another toward holiness.

Paul gives us a model when he rebukes Peter for not eating with Gentiles and influencing Barnabas to do the same. This was Peter returning to the old ways of living by the law. Paul spoke up, not to shame him, but to call him back into alignment with the gospel (Galatians 2:11-21). Peter's behavior was misleading others, so Paul confronted it, not harshly, but honestly. That is what godly conduct does. It is not passive. It speaks when silence would condone sin. It acts when inaction would enable harm.

Scripture makes this calling clear:

"If your brother or sister sins, go and point out their fault, just between the two of you…" - Matthew 18:15 NRSV

"My brothers and sisters, if one of you should wander from the truth and someone should bring that person back, remember this: whoever turns a sinner from the error of their way will save them from death and cover over a multitude of sins." - James 5:19–20 NRSV

This is not about superiority; it is about stewardship. We are not only called to walk in integrity for ourselves. We are called to love others enough to help them walk in it too.

37

The earliest Baptist communities practiced covenantal accountability as a sign of spiritual maturity. If someone sinned openly and refused correction, the community would first approach them privately. If repentance did not follow, they would return with witnesses. Only as a last resort would the person be removed from the community; not out of cruelty, but to awaken repentance and guard the witness of the body.

Today, many avoid confrontation in the name of grace, while others weaponize truth without love. Christ offers another way: correction rooted in compassion, discipline that leads to restoration, and accountability aimed at wholeness. Let your conduct reflect that kind of leadership.

Be someone whose life not only honors God privately but also helps others realign with Him publicly. Lead with truth, seasoned with grace. Speak the hard word when needed, on a foundation of love. Your conduct is not only about personal character; it is about relational discipleship. How you live can point someone else back to Jesus.

For this reason, live well. Speak the truth. Restore gently. Let your example prepare the way for love.

The Sound of Grace

Grace has a sound. It is not loud, harsh, or demeaning. It speaks with gentleness, patience, and affirmation. Grace knows how to tell the truth without crushing someone's spirit. Even in moments of correction, grace preserves a person's dignity. We see this modeled in Jesus. When He corrected Peter, He did not condemn him. When He confronted the woman at the well, He revealed her truth without stripping her of worth. Grace is never passive, yet it is always compassionate.

What if your leadership sounded more like Jesus? What if your voice carried the cadence of grace He used when He interacted with the hurting, the broken, and even the stubborn? Imagine offering a correction that restores rather than humiliates. Imagine leading in a way that strengthens a person's identity rather than diminishing it. That is the leadership Jesus modeled; not weakness, but strength under control.

Consider what it would look like to respond to betrayal the way Jesus did, not with bitterness or revenge, but with holy restraint. On the cross, Jesus had every reason to curse those who crucified Him, instead, He said, *"Father, forgive them, for they know not what they are doing." Luke 23:34 NRSV.* That kind of leadership requires deep trust in God's justice. Holding your tongue does not mean you are afraid; it means you have faith that God is still in control. That restraint becomes a spiritual force, protecting relationships and preserving peace.

Now imagine the kind of team, family, or community that could flourish under leadership like that. A place where people are not afraid to fail because they know failure will not define them. A place where correction is expected, but shame is never part of the process. A place where truth is spoken in love and where grace is not a weakness, but a powerful foundation. That is the kind of culture Jesus built and the kind of culture we are called to create.

The Danger of Idle Words

Matthew 12:36 NIV says, *"Everyone will have to give account on the day of judgment for every empty word they have spoken."* That is not only a verse to memorize; it is a call to deep reflection. Verses like this bring silence to a room. They remind us that God is not only paying attention to our actions, but also to our conversations: the things we say when we are tired, frustrated, trying to be funny, or not thinking.

Idle words are dangerous because they are subtle. They slip out when our guards are down. They show up as throwaway comments we claim "we did not mean." They hide behind the mask of venting, joking, or "just being real." God sees the motive behind every word. Even when we wrap gossip in the language of concern, i.e. "I just wanted to pray for her", He discerns the heart behind it. Even when we tell jokes to fit in or cast shade just to get a laugh, those words still carry weight in the spirit.

We must never forget that both God and the enemy are listening. God hears and records our words because they reflect the condition of our hearts. The enemy looks for openings: words that give him access, fuel division, or plant seeds of doubt, fear, or insecurity. Our words do not disappear into thin air. They create momentum in the spirit. They launch things: blessings or backlash, unity or confusion, healing or harm.

If every conversation is an opportunity to glorify God or grieve Him, then we, as leaders, do not have the luxury of careless speech. Our words carry influence. Let them build. Let them heal. Let them align with the heart of God. One day, we will have to account for every one.

Healing Through Repentance

If this chapter has convicted you, good. Conviction is a gift. It is not condemnation; it is an invitation. When God convicts, it is never to shame or disqualify you. It is to realign you with His heart and His standard. Conviction is proof that your heart is still soft, responsive, and willing to be molded. Leaders who grow are leaders who listen when the Holy Spirit nudges them and say, "Lord, help me do better."

Ask the Holy Spirit to bring to mind the people you have wounded with your words, intentionally or unintentionally. Do not rush this part. Sit with it. Let names and faces rise gently to the surface. Once they do, write them down. This is not about dredging up guilt. It is about making room for healing. Pray for courage to reach out. Pray for wisdom to speak with humility. When the moment comes, do not overexplain. Do not defend. Do not water it down.

Be specific. Be honest. Be kind. Say what needs to be said:

"I realize my words were harsh. I am sorry."

"I see now that I dismissed you instead of listening. Please forgive me."

"I used sarcasm when I should have spoken with care."

"I judged instead of encouraged. That was not fair to you."

A sincere apology goes a long way. It does not erase the wound, but it starts the healing.

You would be surprised how many relationships can be restored with humble words. Grace-filled leaders are not the ones who never mess up. They are the ones who clean it up when they do. They take responsibility. They seek restoration. They value people over pride. That kind of leadership is both rare and powerful. It starts with a single step: letting God clean up your speech so He can work through your voice.

Your Voice Is Needed

Let me be clear: watching your tongue does not mean staying silent when something is wrong. Your voice has a purpose, and silence is not always holy. There are times when love requires boldness. You were given a voice to advocate for the vulnerable, to protect what is sacred, to warn others of danger, to teach truth, and to inspire hope. Scripture is full of men and women who spoke up, not to stir conflict, but to usher in change.

Jesus flipped tables when the temple was being misused, and His passion was fueled by zeal for His Father's house. Paul confronted Peter when his actions were out of step with the gospel. Esther risked everything to speak up for her people, knowing silence would cost lives. These were not moments of pride or performance; they were moments of righteous alignment. Their actions were bold, and their motives were pure. They did not speak to shame; they spoke to restore.

That is the difference. Speaking up in love means your heart is tethered to God's. It means you have checked your motives before releasing your message. Before confronting, correcting, or challenging, ask yourself: Will this build someone up? Will this reflect God's love? Will it bring clarity or confusion? Is this about healing or about proving a point?

Not every strong word is wrong, but every strong word must be surrendered to God first. Before you speak, ask yourself, Are my words rooted in love, truth, and discernment? If the answer is yes, speak with courage. Let your voice carry the strength of wisdom and the gentleness of compassion.

If the answer is no, wait. Do not rush truth without grace, and do not confuse urgency with obedience. Wisdom does not expire. Sometimes the holiest act requires silence until your heart aligns with God's.

You Carry Kingdom Language

God created the world with words. Jesus healed with words. The apostles preached with words. That same creative power rests in your tongue, shaping worlds through your everyday speech. So speak life boldly and wisely.

Let your words correct in love, affirm with intention, and resist sarcasm and gossip. Speak blessings over dry bones, reminding people of who they are in God, even when they forget. You have been given authority not only to lead but to speak as one sent by the King. Let every conversation reflect the Kingdom and every sentence drip with grace. When in doubt, speak less, listen more, and pray always.

Scriptures for the Journey

Take time this week to read these verses slowly. Choose one to memorize, meditate on, or write in your journal as a reminder of who God has called you to be.

Moses said to the Lord, "O my Lord, I have never been eloquent, neither in the past nor even now that you have spoken to your servant; but I am slow of speech and slow of tongue." Then the Lord said to him, "Who gives speech to mortals? Who makes them mute or deaf, seeing or blind? Is it not I, the Lord?" — Exodus 4:10–11 NRSV

The tongue has the power of life and death, and those who love it will eat its fruit. — Proverbs 18:21 NIV

Do not let any unwholesome talk come out of your mouths, but only what is useful for building up, as there is need, so that your words may give grace to those who hear. — Ephesians 4:29 NRSV

Let your speech always be gracious, seasoned with salt, so that you may know how you ought to answer each person. — Colossians 4:6 ESV

I tell you, on the day of judgment people will give an account for every careless word they speak; for by your words you will be justified, and by your words you will be condemned. —
Matthew 12:36–37 ESV

Pause + Reflect

1. When do your words reflect the character of Jesus and when do they not? What environments or relationships tend to bring out the best or the worst in your speech?

2. What is one habit in your speech that needs to change to honor God?

3. This week, who could you intentionally encourage with your words?

Prayer

Heavenly Father,

Please help me live according to Your Word by making my words reflect Your truth and my tone embody Your mercy and grace. Help me be mindful of what I say, that my speech may bless others and never become a tool of harm. As You did with the prophets and with Jesus, give me the right words to speak; words that bring healing, truth, and encouragement to those around me.

I know my tongue holds the power of life and death. Silence me, Lord, when my words are about to tear down what You have built in my spouse, my children, my community, and even within myself. Let my speech always be life-giving and bring You glory.

Grant me wisdom to know what to say and when to say it. Give me peace in moments when You ask me to wait. Write Your Word on my heart so that when I speak, it is Your truth that flows from my mouth to others and back to myself.

Thank You for entrusting me with the authority to lead others toward their identity in You by speaking to them as the beloved children of God that they are. Thank You for Your mercy and grace as I learn to tame my tongue. Please forgive me for words I've spoken that have wounded or torn down others. Help me be a builder in Your Kingdom.

Father, as the psalmist prayed, I ask You:

"Let the words of my mouth and the meditation of my heart be acceptable in Your sight, O Lord, my Strength and my Redeemer." - Psalm 19:14

In Jesus' name,
Amen.

CHAPTER 3

SET AN EXAMPLE IN CONDUCT

"Whatever you have learned or received or heard from me,
or seen in me, put it into practice. And the God of peace
will be with you."
— Philippians 4:9 NIV

It is one thing to speak truth. It is another thing to live it. Your conduct is what makes your leadership believable. People may admire your gifts, but they trust your example. It is not about appearances; it is about alignment. In every space you enter, your character is either confirming your calling or contradicting it. Your conduct is the sermon people remember, and in a culture that rewards image, God is still calling leaders to embody substance.

That is why Paul charged Timothy not only to speak with integrity, but to live with it.

"Set an example for the believers in speech, in conduct, in love, in faith, and in purity" -
1 Timothy 4:12 NIV.

Notice how conduct made the list; because it matters. How we live, how we treat people, how we navigate adversity, it all speaks. Often, it speaks louder than our posts, platforms, or polished church lingo.

Consistency Even in the Bathroom

Conduct is not about titles or visibility. It shows up in how you treat people at the grocery store, at your job, in the carpool line, or while waiting in the doctor's office. It shows up in how you treat the janitor, not just your boss. It shows up when someone cuts you off in traffic or gossips near your desk. Sometimes, it shows up in the most unexpected places, like the bathroom.

In the early days of ministry, I was serving as a children's minister, teaching Sunday school, attending seminary full-time, and just beginning to step into preaching. I was not on the conference circuit. I was not headlining women's events. I was doing the faithful work of preparing lessons, praying over children, and saying yes to the occasional preaching invitation. I was still being formed. When I received an invitation to preach one Sunday, it felt both humbling and exciting.

I arrived early, used the bathroom to wash my hands, and greeted a woman who walked in. She was dressed in Sunday best and, from what I could gather, had grown up in the church and was back visiting family. When I smiled and said hello, she barely acknowledged me. Her energy was dismissive, cold, and uninterested. Then came the plot twist. The same woman watched as I was introduced as the guest preacher and took my seat at the pulpit. The look on her face? Shock.

After the service, she made a beeline to greet me with the biggest smile, suddenly eager to know my name and my story. I was polite, of course, but that experience in the bathroom stayed with me.

Not because I held a grudge, but because it reminded me of something sacred: how we treat people when we think they hold no power tells the truth about our character. You never know who someone is becoming or what assignment God has placed on their life. Leadership is not always loud. Sometimes it wears children's ministry shoes, teaches Sunday school lessons, or washes hands quietly before preaching.

That moment reminded me of a warning found in Scripture, not to judge people based on appearance or status, but to live with humility and consistent love.

"Suppose a man comes into your meeting wearing a gold ring and fine clothes, and a poor man in filthy old clothes also comes in. If you show special attention to the man wearing fine clothes and say, 'Here's a good seat for you,' but say to the poor man, 'You stand there' or 'Sit on the floor by my feet,' have you not discriminated among yourselves and become judges with evil thoughts?" — James 2:2–4, NIV.

We are not called to honor people based on status, style, or perceived importance. We are called to honor them because they are made in the image of God. Your conduct is the sermon people remember. Even in the bathroom.

Walking the Talk

It is easy to quote Scripture. It is harder to live it. We can tell others to forgive, but can we extend grace to someone who betrayed us? We can quote, "Do not be anxious about anything," but do we lay our own worries at Jesus' feet? We can teach patience, but do we trust God in seasons of delay or disappointment?

Anyone can repeat a Bible verse. But leadership is not about reciting, it is about revealing. Conduct is the bridge between what we say and what we believe. When we live the message, we give it power. People stop seeing it as theory and start seeing it as truth.

There is something undeniably powerful about a person who walks with quiet, faithful integrity. I will never forget a woman I served with early in ministry. She was not flashy or loud. She was not constantly trying to be seen. But she was steady. Gentle. Honest. Her presence carried peace. Her word was trustworthy. Her life made me want to know Jesus more, not because she quoted Scripture at me, but because she lived it.

She led without needing attention. She served without demanding applause. Her consistency, over time, built a kind of spiritual authority that could not be imitated.

We underestimate how impactful quiet consistency can be. In a culture obsessed with charisma, God still values character. The fruit of the Spirit is not popularity or perfection, it is *"love, joy, peace, patience, kindness, goodness, faithfulness, gentleness, and self-control"* – Galatians 5:22–23 NIV). These are not traits you perform when the spotlight is on. They are cultivated when no one is watching.

People are not just listening to what we say. They are watching how we live. Does your life affirm what your mouth proclaims? Do your actions match your message? This is why James wrote, *"Do not merely listen to the word, and so deceive yourselves. Do what it says"* (James 1:22 NIV). Integrity is when your walk and your talk tell the same story.

Yes, there will be moments when we fall short. Moments when our humanity gets the best of us. But even then, people will be watching how we respond. Do we make excuses or take responsibility? Do we humble ourselves and seek forgiveness, or do we double down and protect our image?

What people remember most about your leadership is how consistently you live. So, keep walking the talk. Even when no one claps. Even when no one sees. Because your consistency is not in vain. Your life may be the reason someone holds on to hope. And in a world full of noise, your faithfulness might just be the loudest sermon of all.

Conducting Yourself with Grace

Being a leader who operates with the Holy Spirit living inside of them means that as mentors, friends, spouses, and parents, we are called to extend grace. Grace is such a beautiful gift, one we so rarely give away even though we should. If we walked in humility, we would recognize how great the gift of Christ truly is. He died, rose, and justified us.

However, when we excuse our behavior because of position, power, or length of service, we justify actions that do not represent Christ and dismiss what His blood has accomplished for us. The less we remember the grace we receive, the less we will extend it to others.

I speak from experience when I say that extending grace has been a struggle for me as a leader because I believe in accountability and changed behavior. The more I walk with the Holy Spirit, the clearer I see the difference between divine transformation and worldly change. The world seeks change through threats of violence, cancel culture, and shame. God transforms us with His grace and mercy.

Lamentations 3:22-23 (NIV) reminds us, *"Because of the Lord's great love we are not consumed, for His compassions never fail. They are new every morning; great is Your faithfulness."* God gives us time to reflect and correct our behavior with compassion. As we have received, so we must also give. I urge you to do unto others as Christ has done for you. Meet your family, team, and community with compassion, grace, and mercy. When you feel you have given all the grace you can, remember that God continues to give you grace in areas where He still longs to see growth.

What people remember most about your leadership is how consistently and graciously you live. So keep walking the talk, even when no one applauds, even when no one notices, because your consistency is not in vain. Your life may be the reason someone holds on to hope. In a world full of noise, your faithfulness may be the loudest sermon of all.

Conduct in Conflict

How you act in conflict reveals more about your character than any sermon. It is easy to appear holy when everyone agrees with you. But leadership will test your spirit. People will misunderstand you, challenge your decisions, and talk behind your back. In those moments, your response matters more than your defense.

Jesus modeled this. When the Pharisees accused Him, He responded with truth, not retaliation. When Peter denied Him, He restored him. When Judas betrayed Him, He still called him "friend." Godly conduct means choosing humility over vengeance, clarity over chaos, grace over pride. It does not mean you are passive. It means you are surrendered. You lead with the Spirit, not your emotions.

Conflict will come, and when it does, it often exposes the places in us that still need healing. That is why conflict is not just a leadership issue, it is a discipleship opportunity. Will I let the Holy Spirit refine me here, or will I let my flesh take over? Will I guard my tongue, or will I weaponize my words? Will I pray before responding, or will I react out of pride?

Leadership does not exempt you from offense. In fact, it often attracts it. Your reaction in those moments builds your reputation more than your resume ever will. Will people say you lashed out, or that you listened? Will they remember your ego, or your empathy?

Paul wrote, "As far as it depends on you, live at peace with everyone" (Romans 12:18 NIV). That does not mean peace will always be possible, but your conduct should never be the reason it is not. Paul wrote, "As far as it depends on you, live at peace with everyone" (Romans 12:18 NIV). That does not mean peace will always be possible, but your conduct should never be the reason it is not. You may have to speak hard truths, but speak them from a steady place. You may have to draw boundaries, but draw them with integrity, not resentment.

Sometimes the most Christlike response is to remain steady when everything around you feels unstable. Godly conduct is not proven in calm seasons but in chaotic ones. It is seen when you choose patience over provocation, integrity over impulse, and peace over pride.

When conflict arises, let it become a mirror that reflects your formation. Do your actions reveal that you trust God, or that you are still trying to prove yourself? Every disagreement becomes an invitation to demonstrate who leads you. Let your life show that the Spirit governs your reactions. Because true leadership is not measured by how you handle agreement, but by how you conduct yourself when you are tested.

Boundaries Are Biblical

Sometimes we confuse Christlike conduct with people-pleasing. We think being nice means always saying yes, never disappointing anyone, and making room for every request, no matter how draining. That is not what Jesus modeled. His conduct was compassionate, not codependent. He was led by the Spirit, not controlled by others' expectations.

Even Jesus walked away from crowds. He withdrew to pray. He got in the boat and crossed to the other side. He left the ninety-nine to pursue the one, but He also preached shake the dust off His feet when people rejected the message. He didn't chase those who walked away. He did not perform for the approval of people. He honored His assignment, not their applause.

That alone should challenge how we think about boundaries. We often assume boundaries are selfish, cold, or unkind, but in reality, boundaries are holy. Conduct includes knowing when to say yes and when to step back; when to pour out and when to pull away; when to help and when to rest. When we allow our peace to be constantly violated, we become resentful, and resentment clouds our leadership. It hardens our heart and slowly poisons our love.

Jesus showed us that even divine love has limits. He was always loving, but He was not always available. He did not try to be everything to everyone. He moved with discernment, not desperation.

Jesus also showed restraint when the crowd tried to crown Him for the wrong reasons. After feeding the five thousand, the people were amazed, not at His heart, but at His power. They saw the miracle and wanted to make Him king by force. But Jesus did not come to be a provider of convenience. He came to reign in the heart, not to sit on a throne built by human hands.

"Jesus, knowing that they intended to come and make him king by force, withdrew again to a mountain by himself" (John 6:15 NIV).

He walked away, not because He lacked compassion, but because He would not be confined to their expectations. They wanted a king who could multiply bread, not one who would become the Bread of Life. They wanted a crown without the cross. But Jesus chose obedience over affirmation. He slipped away to be alone, guarding the purity of His purpose.

That is what boundary-setting looks like in the kingdom: refusing to trade your calling for applause; refusing to be shaped by the crowd when you are already surrendered to the King.

Saying no is not selfish. It is wise. Boundaries protect your purpose. They guard your joy. They make room for spiritual health. When you are overextended, burned out, and running on empty, you begin leading from exhaustion instead of overflow, and that is not sustainable. That is not ministry, it is self-neglect masquerading as devotion.

It is the burning of an offering God did not require, like the unauthorized fire brought by Aaron's sons. Nadab and Abihu were priests set apart for holy service, but they acted out of presumption instead of obedience. They offered fire God never asked for, stepping outside their assignment and treating the sacred as casual.

"Nadab and Abihu, the sons of Aaron, took their censers, put fire in them and added incense; and they offered unauthorized fire before the Lord, contrary to his command. So fire came out

from the presence of the Lord and consumed them, and they died before the Lord" (Leviticus 10:1–2 NIV).

You were never called to save everyone. You were not built to carry every burden. Jesus is the Savior. You are His servant. Your job is not to be endlessly accessible, but to be faithfully aligned with what God has actually called you to do.

Boundaries also preserve your identity. When you constantly say yes out of guilt, fear, or pressure, you start losing yourself. You stop hearing God clearly because the noise of people's demands becomes louder than the Spirit's voice. You wake up wondering who you are living for, and that is not peace, it is bondage.

Healthy boundaries reflect trust in God. You trust that He will meet the needs you cannot. You trust that He will raise up others to serve when you need to rest. You trust that saying no to them can still mean saying yes to Him.

"Am I now trying to win the approval of human beings, or of God? Or am I trying to please people? If I were still trying to please people, I would not be a servant of Christ" (Galatians 1:10 NIV).

Let that Scripture anchor you. When Paul wrote this to the churches in Galatia, he was not just making a passing statement, he was drawing a line in the sand. False teachers had come in twisting the gospel, adding extra burdens and rules, trying to win approval from religious leaders and make the message more palatable. Paul was not interested in gaining popularity. He was not trying to soften the truth. He was defending the gospel he had received directly from Jesus

Christ, and he made it clear: he could not serve both God and the crowd.

His words remind us that people-pleasing and faithful leadership rarely go hand in hand. If your aim is always to be liked, you will eventually compromise what is right. But if your aim is to please God, you will be misunderstood at times, and that is okay. Paul understood this tension deeply. He had once been a Pharisee, well-respected and admired in religious circles. But once Christ called him, he surrendered his reputation to walk in obedience. That shift cost him popularity, comfort, and control, but it gave him purpose, clarity, and lasting fruit.

For leaders today, especially those called to shepherd others, this verse becomes a gut-check. Who am I really trying to please? Who am I building my schedule, my boundaries, and my energy around, people, or God? Am I driven by guilt or led by the Spirit?

When your life is anchored in God's approval, you are free to set boundaries without shame. You are no longer manipulated by the fear of letting people down, because your identity is secure. You stop chasing every request, because you know your calling is specific. You stop over-functioning, because you trust that God can raise up others to carry the load. You do not have to do everything. You just have to be faithful to what He asked you to do.

That is what Paul modeled, and that is what you are invited into: a life led by conviction, not control. Boundaries rooted in obedience, not performance. Leadership grounded in freedom, not fear.

Boundaries are not about building walls to keep people out. They are about building margins that help you stay spiritually, emotionally, and physically well. They protect your ability to love people deeply without losing yourself completely. That is what Jesus modeled.

He did not let pressure dictate His pace. He did not sacrifice obedience on the altar of urgency. He knew when to retreat. He knew when to rest. He trusted that His mission would still move forward.

Take a deep breath. Let go of the guilt. You are allowed to rest. You are allowed to have limits.

You are allowed to step back without stepping away from love. Boundaries do not make you unkind. They make you wise. Boundaries protect your purpose.

When You Fall Short

You will mess up. We all do. What matters is how you respond.

Leadership does not mean getting it right every time. Sometimes it means owning when you do not. Godly leaders take responsibility. They apologize without manipulation. They ask for feedback and grow through correction.

I have learned this the hard way, more than once. My tone has not always reflected my heart. My delivery has sometimes wounded more than my intention ever meant to. I can think of moments when I lost patience with people I was called to shepherd.

One of my favorite ways to minister is through small groups and book studies. I have facilitated them in churches, universities, and even with friends. One time, while leading a small group, there was an individual who frequently interrupted, challenged the flow of discussion, and often made it difficult for others to engage. After several months of trying to navigate it with grace, I reached a point where, in a moment of frustration, I said, "If you do not want to be here, you do not have to come."

Looking back, I wish I had paused, prayed, and found a more gracious way to address it. The situation reminded me how easy it is to let frustration lead when I have not been refilled in private. Was I wrong for correcting him? No. But my tone lacked grace.

The frustration had built up without being released in prayer, and instead of leading, I reacted. That moment taught me something: I see how Moses missed the Promised Land. Leading people is beautiful, but it is also hard. You can be anointed and still feel frustrated at times. You can love the people you shepherd, and they can still get on your nerves.

I say this not to discredit my leadership, but to be honest about it. Some of the most defining moments in my growth were the moments I had to repent to Jesus and ask a brother or sister for forgiveness.

For a long time, those moments haunted me. I hated falling short. I did not want to disappoint anyone, especially

Jesus. I wanted to be a perfect leader so I could prove to others, and to myself, that I was worthy of him calling me. I wanted to lead well, speak wisely, and walk with integrity.

I eventually had to confront the lie that said I had to get everything right to be effective. Because the truth is, you can say all the right things and still miss someone's expectations. You can show up with a surrendered heart and still get misunderstood. You can pray to be a great minister, coach, or teacher and still have someone not choose to follow your leadership. Leadership is not about being flawless. It is about being faithful.

I learned this lesson one day when God used my favorite athlete, Serena Williams, to teach me something I did not even know I needed. I was watching one of her matches. She missed a return. Then a serve. She even lost a set. But in the end, she still won the championship.

Serena's track record is extraordinary. She won 23 major championships and took home more than 70 career titles over the course of her career. She has been ranked number one in the world more than once and is widely considered one of the greatest athletes of all time. And still, she has never played a perfect match.

God used that moment to show me something simple but profound: you can mess up and still come out victorious. Serena has never played a perfect game, but that has never stopped her from becoming one of the greatest athletes of all time. Your mistakes don't disqualify you from becoming the leader God called you to be.

If Serena can train for years, put in the work, make mistakes, and still win the prize, then how much more should we hold onto grace when we fall short in our own race? Paul reminds us, *"Everyone who competes in the games goes into strict training. They do it to get a crown that will not last, but we do it to get a crown that will last forever"* (1 Corinthians 9:25, NIV).

When we are living by the Spirit and leading in the name of Christ, we may miss the mark at times, but God's grace is sufficient. Even when we fall short, we are not disqualified. We can still finish well. We can still receive the crown.

When you fall short, let it be an invitation, not an indictment. Let it be the beginning of deeper healing and wiser leadership. Some of your greatest influence may come not from how well you teach, but how humbly you repent.

Conduct That Impacts Generations

You may think your conduct only affects you. It does not. Someone is always watching. A younger sibling might be imitating your patience or your sarcasm.

A student might be studying how you lead under pressure. A coworker might be learning how to forgive based on how you model grace. A child might be learning how to talk to others by watching how you treat strangers. The next generation does not just need our advice; they need our example.

Words fade, but habits leave a mark. People may not remember every teaching, but they will remember how you handled pain; how you loved when it was hard; how you stood firm in seasons of testing. Your conduct becomes their curriculum. Your consistency becomes their compass. So, live like someone is learning from your footsteps, because they are. Jesus did.

Living Epistles

Scripture says we are living letters, *"known and read by everyone"* 2 Corinthians 3:2–3. You do not need a microphone or a ministry title to share the gospel. Your life is already preaching. Your tone, your timing, your reactions, your priorities, all of it speaks. From time to time, stop and ask: What is my life saying?

People are not just listening to what you say. They are watching how you live. You are a walking sermon. Let your life be so filled with Christ that even your silence points people to Him.

Scriptures for the Journey

Take time this week to read these verses slowly. Choose one to memorize, meditate on, or write in your journal as a reminder of who God has called you to be.

In all your ways acknowledge Him, and He shall direct your paths. — Proverbs 3:6 NKJV

And when you turn to the right or when you turn to the left, your ears shall hear a word behind you, saying, "This is the way; walk in it." — Isaiah 30:21 NRSV

For you have been called to live in freedom, my brothers and sisters. But do not use your freedom to satisfy your sinful nature. Instead, use your freedom to serve one another in love. — Galatians 5:13 NLT

For we are God's handiwork, created in Christ Jesus to do good works, which God prepared in advance for us to do. — Ephesians 2:10 NIV

Whatever happens, conduct yourselves in a manner worthy of the gospel of Christ. — Philippians 1:27 NIV

Pause + Reflect

1. Are there areas where your actions do not line up with your faith? What are they?

2. Who in your life inspires you by the way they live out their beliefs?

3. What's one practical habit you can begin this week to reflect Christ more clearly?

Prayer

Father,

Please help me live out what I believe both behind closed doors and in public.
Bury Your Word deep in my heart, and open my eyes and ears to hear Your Spirit speak.
Make me someone You can trust to be a blessing to Your people.

When You give me power, help me to steward it with humility. When You give me vision, give me the character to see it through. When You pour out Your grace and mercy upon me, teach me to give it freely to others.

I pray that when people see me, they see You.
Let everything I do bring You glory.

In Jesus' name,
Amen.

CHAPTER 4

SET AN EXAMPLE IN LOVE

"This is my commandment, that you love one another as I have loved you."
— John 15:12 (ESV)

As leaders, we must lead with compassion, grace, and truth. When Paul exhorted Timothy to be an example *"in speech, in conduct, in love, in faith, and in purity,"* love was not just one among many, love was central. Without love, leadership becomes performance. Without love, influence becomes manipulation. Without love, we may move crowds, but we will never move hearts. Love is the fuel of godly leadership, and it is the ultimate marker of spiritual maturity.

Love: The True Mark of a Disciple

In John 13:34–35, Jesus delivers a powerful and transformative command: *"Love one another. As I have loved you, so you must love one another. By this everyone will know that you are my disciples if you love one another."* This instruction was not a suggestion or an idealistic theory, it was a directive tied directly to our identity as followers of Christ. Love is the distinguishing mark of a disciple. Not eloquence. Not accomplishments. Not charisma. Love.

Jesus warned that in the last days, many would claim to have served Him, *prophesying, casting out demons, even performing miracles but still be unknown to Him* (Matthew 7:22–23 NIV). That sobering truth reminds us that the goal was never performance. The goal was always relationship. Love is not proven by charisma, charm or how many Bible verses you have memorized. It is proven by our heart posture, our obedience, and the way we live out His presence in our daily lives. The world may applaud power and platform, but heaven recognizes love.

Godly love is not based on how much we agree, how much we have in common, or how well someone treats us. It's sacrificial. It costs something. It looks like showing up for someone who cannot return the favor. It looks like keeping your heart soft after betrayal. It looks like choosing to believe the best, even when the evidence suggests otherwise. Love requires maturity, intention, and the power of the Holy Spirit.

In a world that often confuses love with tolerance or attraction, Christian leaders are called to embody something deeper, *agape*. This love forgives before it is asked, serves before it is thanked, and gives without expecting return. It challenges injustice, uplifts the broken, and reflects the heart of Jesus in every interaction. Love is extending new mercies to others each day, just as God faithfully pours them out on you. If we want to be known as His disciples, we must start by loving as He did: radically, relentlessly, and unconditionally.

Jesus: Love in Action

Jesus was love in human form. Every miracle He performed, every parable He told, every rebuke He gave, even His moments of silence, were saturated with love. His actions were not random acts of kindness or mere demonstrations of power; they were expressions of divine compassion. Love was not just what He showed, it was who He was. Everything He did reflected the Father's heart.

One of the most powerful examples of this is found in John 8, when a woman caught in adultery was brought before Jesus. The Pharisees did not care about her well-being or redemption; they wanted to use her as a trap to discredit Jesus. Legally, she could have been stoned. But Jesus, fully aware of both *justice* and *mercy*, responded with unmatched wisdom and compassion. *"Let him who is without sin cast the first stone,"* he said. One by one, her accusers disappeared, silenced not just by truth but by love. Then Jesus turned to her and said, *"Neither do I condemn you. Go, and sin no more."* He did not excuse her actions, but He did not discard her either. That is redemptive love, truthful, and tender.

This moment teaches us that love does not mean ignoring wrongdoing; it means responding to it with grace. Jesus never watered down righteousness, but He always paired it with mercy. His love was not permissive, it was transformative. He did not shame people into holiness; He loved them into it.

That kind of love is uncomfortable for the proud and healing for the broken. It invites repentance without ridicule and offers a way forward instead of a final judgment.

Jesus also loved those society rejected. He embraced the leper, called the Samaritan woman worthy, and called the unseen by name. He turned the rejected woman at the well into a witness, and her testimony drew an entire village to believe. He called Zacchaeus down from a tree and transformed a corrupt tax collector into a generous disciple. He also chose shepherds, often distrusted and looked down upon as unclean, to be the first to receive heaven's announcement of His birth. And He called fishermen, common laborers with no formal education or influence, to walk closely with Him and carry His message to the world.

His love challenged the powerful and embraced the powerless. He was present with people others avoided. His model of love reminds us that true love means availability, compassion, and courage. As leaders and disciples, we are called to mirror this kind of love: active, unshakable, and present, even when it is inconvenient.

Paul and Barnabas: Love That Believes in Others

Paul is a powerful example of someone who was loved into leadership. Before becoming the apostle who wrote much of the New Testament, he was Saul, a man known for hunting down and persecuting Christians. His name struck fear in the hearts of believers, and his reputation was built on violence and opposition to the very gospel he would later preach. After his dramatic conversion on the road to Damascus, most early Christians were understandably skeptical. They doubted the authenticity of his transformation, and many wanted nothing to do with him.

But Barnabas saw something different. Known in Scripture as the "Son of Encouragement" (Acts 4:36), Barnabas chose to believe in the work God was doing in Paul's life. While others distanced themselves, Barnabas stepped in, advocated for Paul, and stood beside him. Acts 9:26–27 tells us that when Paul came to Jerusalem and tried to join the disciples, they were afraid of him. But *Barnabas took him to the apostles, shared Paul's testimony, and vouched for the sincerity of his faith.* Barnabas' support was not just an act of kindness, it was an act of leadership. His willingness to love, trust, and affirm Paul opened the door for one of the greatest ministries in church history.

This example raises an important question for today's leaders: Are we the kind of people who offer grace when it is risky? Do we believe in others when it is unpopular to do so? Being an example in love does not always look like grand gestures or emotional words. It means choosing not to hold someone hostage to who they were but instead calling them forward into who they are becoming. It is easy to stand with people when their transformation is complete. It takes faith to stand with them while they are still becoming.

Barnabas' love became the bridge between Paul's past and his purpose. But it was not blind trust, it was Spirit-led wisdom. He discerned what God was doing in Paul's life and responded with courageous love.

Love Requires Wisdom

Being an example in love does not mean becoming a doormat. Too often, love is misunderstood as passivity, allowing others to walk over you in the name of kindness or peace. But the love Jesus modeled was anything but passive. He loved deeply, sacrificially, and consistently, but He also demonstrated wisdom in how He gave of Himself. Jesus withdrew from crowds when He needed rest. He took time to pray alone. He did not chase after people who were only interested in His miracles. John 2:24–25 tells us, *"But Jesus would not entrust himself to them, for he knew all people. He did not need any testimony about mankind, for he knew what was in each person."* His love was powerful, but it was not naive.

True love has boundaries. Love is not obligated to say yes to everything or tolerate behavior that dishonors God or devalues others. Sometimes love says no, not out of hardness, but out of holiness. Saying no to manipulation, abuse, or toxic behavior is not unloving; it is wise. Jesus did not allow people to use Him, and we should not either. A loving leader does not enable dysfunction, they lovingly confront it or step away when needed. This takes discernment and courage, but it is often the most loving response.

Love, when healthy, respects both the giver and the recipient. It is not one-sided or self-sacrificing to the point of burnout. Healthy love creates space for growth, accountability, and mutual honor. It does not thrive in codependency or fear. It invites truth and fosters trust. If your love leaves you constantly drained, constantly overlooked, or constantly compromising your values, then it is time to ask: is this truly love, or is this people-pleasing in disguise?

Do not confuse love with the need to be liked. People-pleasing seeks approval. Love seeks what is best. Love does not just keep the peace, it makes peace. It has the boldness to speak the truth, the strength to walk away when necessary, and the grace to do both with compassion. As a leader, you are not called to be everyone's favorite, you are called to be faithful. And sometimes, the most faithful, loving thing you can do is honor your limits and walk in truth.

Wise love knows when to draw boundaries and when to draw near. That is exactly what Ruth did.

Ruth: Loyalty as Love

Ruth's love for Naomi stands as one of the most beautiful and selfless examples of sacrificial love in all of Scripture. After losing her husband, Ruth was under no cultural or legal obligation to remain with Naomi, her mother-in-law. Naomi even encouraged her to return to her people and start a new life. But Ruth's response is legendary in its devotion: *"Where you go, I will go. Where you stay, I will stay. Your people will be my people and your God my God"* (Ruth 1:16, NIV). Her words were not just a declaration of loyalty, they were a covenant of love. She chose to bind her life to Naomi's, not for gain, but out of deep, unwavering care.

What makes Ruth's decision so remarkable is that it was made in the face of uncertainty. She was not choosing a path of ease or opportunity. She was aligning herself with a grieving, aging woman with no guarantees of provision, status, or security. But true love does not demand conditions. It doesn't ask, "What's in it for me?" Ruth did not calculate the cost, she simply loved. In doing so, she demonstrated the kind of covenant love that mirrors God's own heart.

Ruth's love did more than comfort Naomi, it revived her hope. Through Ruth's loyalty, Naomi witnessed God's faithfulness again and was restored from bitterness to joy. Ruth was also blessed. Her faithfulness eventually led her to Boaz, a man of integrity and compassion who became her husband. But even more significantly, Ruth became the great-grandmother of King David, and her name was forever grafted into the genealogy of Jesus Christ. Her story reminds us that acts of love, even in obscurity, carry generational weight. Sacrificial love is not just a feeling, it is a force that reshapes destiny.

In a world that often prioritizes individual success and personal advancement, Ruth's story stands in contrast. It shows us that love can do what ambition cannot. Ruth did not chase influence, she followed love. And in doing so, God opened doors no résumé ever could. Her legacy teaches us that when we lead with love, especially love that costs us something, we align ourselves with heaven's purposes. It is not always the most strategic move in the eyes of the world, but in God's economy, love is always the most powerful investment.

Love That Honors the Mission

John the Baptist and Jesus shared a holy and prophetic connection that modeled humility, honor, and divine alignment. Though John had his own thriving ministry, drawing crowds, baptizing multitudes, and boldly proclaiming repentance, he knew his role was not to be the center of the story. John recognized the supremacy of Jesus and declared, *"After me comes one who is more powerful than I, the straps of whose sandals I am not worthy to stoop down and untie"* (Mark 1:7 NIV). This was not just deference. It was spiritual clarity. John's love and loyalty to God's plan compelled him to decrease so Christ could be magnified.

John's actions reveal that godly love in leadership is not self-preserving. Though he had influence, he never let pride take root. When his own disciples became concerned that more people were going to Jesus, John responded without jealousy or defensiveness: *"He must increase, but I must decrease"* (John 3:30 KJV)). He understood that his assignment was to prepare the way, not to block the path. In a world obsessed with platform and visibility, John shows us what it looks like to release control and rejoice in someone else's rise, not out of obligation but out of reverence and love for the mission of God.

In leadership, especially in competitive spaces, it can be tempting to cling to influence or resent those who grow beyond us. But John the Baptist shows us a more excellent way. Love is not threatened by someone else's anointing. It does not panic when others step into their calling. True love makes room. John did not just acknowledge Jesus. He pointed people to Him. He fulfilled his calling by ensuring the people looked not to him but to the Lamb of God who takes away the sin of the world. That is what love looks like in leadership: humility that protects, honors, and yields.

Love in leadership means preparing the way for others to walk in their divine purpose, even when that means stepping out of the spotlight. It is the kind of love that paves roads, blesses transitions, and trusts God's timing over personal gain. John the Baptist teaches us that the goal is not to remain the loudest voice but to be faithful to the voice of God. And in the Kingdom, those who clear the way, those who lead in love, are the ones who help usher in the presence of Christ for generations to come.

When Love Costs You Something

Love is often romanticized in our culture, portrayed as effortless, glamorous, and always convenient. It looks like curated Instagram captions, fairytale proposals, and relationships that never require hard conversations. But biblical love tells a different story. Real love costs. It cost Jesus everything. It required Him to leave the comfort of heaven, endure rejection, suffer injustice, and give His life so we could be restored to the Father. That same kind of sacrificial love is what we are called to embody. It might cost you your comfort, your pride, your right to "clap back," or your need to always be understood. Love often calls us to take the high road when everything in us craves justice on our own terms. It invites us to be quiet when we want to have the last word and to forgive when we would rather hold a grudge.

Love Leaves an Eternal Mark

The fruit of leading with love often reaches further than we realize. Love leaves an imprint that no position or title ever could. People may admire your gifts or appreciate your knowledge, but it is your love that softens hearts and builds trust. It is not the eloquence of your sermons that lingers, it is the compassion in your silence, the patience in your presence, and the grace in your words. People remember who made them feel seen. They remember who showed up. In that remembrance, they catch a glimpse of the God who never leaves.

That kind of love shifts atmospheres. It disarms hostility. It builds trust.

Scriptures for the Journey

Take time this week to read these verses slowly. Choose one to memorize, meditate on, or write in your journal as a reminder of who God has called you to be.

"This is my commandment, that you love one another as I have loved you." — John 15:12 (NRSV)

"Let love be genuine; hate what is evil, hold fast to what is good. Love one another with mutual affection; outdo one another in showing honor." — Romans 12:9–10 (NRSV)

"Whoever wants to be first must be last of all and servant of all." — Mark 9:35 (NRSV)

"Above all, clothe yourselves with love, which binds everything together in perfect harmony." — Colossians 3:14 (NRSV)

"The greatest among you will be your servant." — Matthew 23:11 (NRSV)

Pause + Reflect

1. When you think about the way Jesus loved, what stands out most to you? How does that challenge you?

2. In what ways do you struggle with showing love when it is inconvenient, uncomfortable, or unreciprocated?

3. How can your daily life reflect a love that is rooted in truth, not just kindness or emotion?

Prayer

Holy Spirit,

I can love others because You first loved me. Because You forgave me, I can forgive. As I have freely received from You, help me to pour it out generously onto those around me.

Your love changed my life and gave me my identity. *Your love is patient and kind. It does not envy, boast, or dishonor others.*

It is not proud, self-seeking, or easily angered. It keeps no record of wrongs. Your love does not delight in evil but rejoices with the truth. It always protects, always trusts, always hopes, always perseveres. Your love never fails (1 Corinthians 13:4-8 NIV). Thank You for loving me with that kind of love.

While I was still a sinner, You sent Your Son to redeem me. Help me to love others with that same grace, not because they have earned it, but because You gave it to me. I repent for the times I have made my love conditional. Forgive me for withholding love out of fear, pride, bias, or anger.

Teach me to love without limits. Help me to show compassion to my neighbors, my teammates, the outsider, and even those who disagree with me. As I have received, so I will give.

Thank You for loving all You have created. Help me to love like You.

In Jesus' name,
Amen.

CHAPTER 5

SET AN EXAMPLE IN FAITH

"Have I not commanded you? Be strong and courageous. Do not be afraid; do not be discouraged, for the Lord your God will be with you wherever you go."
— Joshua 1:9 NIV

The Texas heat hit hard that summer after my first semester of seminary. I had dreams of lazy pool days and weekends with friends, but life had other plans. My car gave out. The air conditioning in my apartment broke, and both were beyond repair. I found myself unexpectedly hunting for a new place to live and a new vehicle, all before classes resumed.

"You've got to be kidding me," I whispered to no one in particular, staring at the unmoving ceiling fan. But this was real. There was no reset button.

I prayed, reached out to mentors, and slowly, things came together. A new apartment closer to campus, a roommate, and a reliable car. Everything aligned just in time. I exhaled. Life, it seemed, was settling.

Faith Begins with Confidence in God

One of the clearest pictures of faith in Scripture comes from the story of David and Goliath. David was just a shepherd boy when he volunteered to fight a trained Philistine warrior. Saul offered him royal, custom-made armor, but David turned it down.

"I have never used this," he said. "I cannot go in it."

David's faith was not in weapons or titles. It was in God. As he stood before Goliath, he declared:

"You come to me with sword and spear and javelin, but I come to you in the name of the Lord of hosts" (1 Samuel 17:45 ESV). And with a single stone and unwavering trust in God, the giant fell.

Why God Is Worthy of Our Faith

Faith grows when we know who God is. The more clearly, we see His character, the more freely we can trust His heart. Before we examine how Jesus lived by faith, we must pause and remember who this God is that we are invited to believe.

He is not distant or impersonal. He is not moody or manipulative. He is the same yesterday, today, and forever. He is holy and good, powerful and patient. He has always been faithful. He cannot lie. He does not fail.

Following the Faith *of* Christ

The more I studied faith, the more I realized Jesus did not just invite people to believe in God. He showed us how. His whole life was a pattern of trust. Every miracle, every moment of ministry, every quiet prayer revealed what it looks like to walk in full dependence on the Father.

During my undergraduate studies, one of my professors introduced a concept that shifted my perspective completely. We were reading through the letters of Paul when he paused and asked us to consider a small phrase with a big impact: "the faith *of* Jesus Christ."

At the time, I had never paid much attention to the wording. But in certain translations, especially the King James Version, that phrase appears exactly as it is: not faith in Jesus Christ, but the faith of Jesus Christ. That distinction matters.

> "… *the righteousness of God which is* **by faith of Jesus Christ** *unto all and upon all them that believe* … " — Romans 3:22 (KJV)
>
> "… *that we might be justified* **by the faith of Christ,** *and not by the works of the law…* " — Galatians 2:16 (KJV)

Modern translations often say "faith in Christ" to emphasize our belief in Him, which is true and important. But the original Greek allows for both readings: our faith in Jesus and the faith of Jesus Himself. In other words, we are not only saved by believing in Him. We are invited to live with the same faith He lived by.

Jesus did not cling to comfort or certainty. He chose obedience over ease. From the moment He left heaven to the final moments on the cross, He modeled trust. He embraced the limitations of human life, knowing full well the cost. When faced with betrayal, rejection, and unimaginable suffering, He leaned on the Father again and again.

Even in Gethsemane, when sorrow pressed Him to the ground, His faith did not waver. "Not My will, but Yours be done," He prayed. That is what faith looks like; not just trusting in what God can do, but surrendering to who God is, even when the outcome is painful.

Jesus was able to trust fully because He came from the Father and knew the presence of God, and because of His death and resurrection, we have that same access to God through the Holy Spirit. Sometimes we assume that of course Jesus trusted God. He is divine. But what He showed us was how to live in full surrender as a human being filled with the Spirit.

Now, by the same Spirit, we have been made new. We are no longer just descendants of Adam. We belong to Christ. His identity is ours. His righteousness is ours. His faith can be ours too.

Live *By* Faith

Faith is not only something we believe; it is something we live. It is more than a theological idea, it is the lens through which we see and respond to the world. As Paul affirms in Romans 1:17, *"The just shall live by faith."* This is not a momentary decision, but a continual posture. Faith shapes our words, informs our choices, and steadies us when the path is unclear. It says, "Even when I do not understand, I trust the One who does."

Living by faith means obeying before we have all the answers. It is rising with questions but still choosing to walk. It is trusting God's timing when we feel forgotten. Faith is not passive, it leans forward. It does not rely on a roadmap but on relationship.

The story of Lazarus illustrates this beautifully; it shows us what happens when faith meets the voice of Jesus. When Jesus finally arrived in Bethany, Lazarus had already been dead for four days. His sisters, Mary and Martha, were deep in grief, convinced that all hope was lost. From a human standpoint, it was over. But faith does not stop where human reasoning does. Jesus told them to roll away the stone, a bold and bewildering request. But the people did it anyways. Then He called Lazarus by name, and the man who had been buried stepped out of the tomb alive (John 11:1–44).

Where others see a grave, faith sees a door. This is the invitation of faith. To believe even when everything looks final. To trust that God can speak life where others see only loss. When you live by faith, you do not deny what is hard, you stand in it, anchored by the truth that Jesus always has the final word. When you live by faith, you will witness God breathe life into things you thought were finished.

Trust Through the Uncertain

Before seminary, I spent five years teaching. The first two were in New York, then internationally, in Venezuela and Guatemala. Where I loved living and teaching but through prayer, God called me to back to the United States. I returned to my hometown and taught Spanish at a Catholic school while pursuing my second Bachelor's degree in Religion and Philosophy. Once I completed my degree program, God led me to Baylor's Truett Seminary.

I enrolled full-time, served as an associate pastor at Greater Bosqueville Baptist Church and held a graduate assistantship in the recruitment office at the seminary. But then after being in the recruitment position for nearly a year, God asked me to leave that role and I had no backup plan.

By January, I had completed a full year of seminary. My roommate let me know she would be moving out when our lease ended in July. I could not afford the apartment alone. The ground beneath me felt unstable. All I could do was pray.

I reached out to my pastor, Reverend Ron L. English. "I need help discerning my next season," I told him. He walked with me through that uncertain space with wisdom and calm. By the spring semester, I had applied to several jobs, everything from a summer camp to a family-owned pizza shop in Waco. I just needed income.

I did receive callbacks from all of them and by April narrowed it down to two: one with Baylor's School of Education for a graduate assistant role reviewing student-teacher portfolios and another for a chaplain position in an addiction recovery program on campus. Both were meaningful opportunities. I was prepared to say yes to whichever door opened first.

The graduate assistant job in the Baylor School of Education was my first interview. Just getting the interview was a credit to Dr. Hulitt Gloer, my preaching professor at Truett, who had graciously referred me. I walked in thinking I would be discussing clerical tasks and student portfolio management. The role paid $8 an hour, and in my head, I was already wondering how in the world I was going to make ends meet on that.

What I did not know was that the decision had already been made before I arrived. The interview was a formality. They had reviewed my résumé in advance and had already decided to offer me something completely different: an adjunct professor position. My mouth dropped. It paid more and was aligned with everything I had dreamed of.

While living overseas, I had led and facilitated workshops for teachers, and I loved mentoring new educators. The chance to train first-year teachers in a university setting felt like an answered prayer. I was stunned, humbled, and grateful until I walked out the door and heard God say no.

After hearing the no, I was disappointed, but it was fine. I already had another interview lined up with the addiction recovery program on campus for a chaplain position.

I was not entirely sure I was qualified, but since God had just closed one door, I wondered if this might be the one He was opening. Maybe it would stretch me in ways I needed. I was uncertain, but I showed up. When I arrived, I was interviewed by a small panel. Two or three people were in the room asking questions and taking notes. I answered as best I could, not knowing what would come next.

Not long after that panel interview, I received an unexpected phone call from one of the interviewers offering me another opportunity. She also oversaw Baylor's Resident Chaplain program and shared that they had been searching for the right person to fill a unique role. One of the communities, an apartment-style residence for upper-division students slightly off campus had remained unfilled since January. The students there included international students, first-year athletes, and transfers.

I could not ignore the alignment. When I started college, I attended community college, then transferred to a university. I studied abroad while earning my bachelor's degree, and I played basketball all four years of college. In so many ways, I was being called to serve the kind of student I had once been.

She told me there were normally several rounds of interviews, but she would count this one. That same week, I met with the residence hall director. Within days, I was offered the position. The role came with a stipend, free housing, and a meal plan; everything I needed. It started right as my lease was ending. I was stunned by the timing, but more than that, I was moved by the invitation. This was not just a job. It was a call to lead in a way I had never experienced before. Over 500 students from dozens of nations and faith backgrounds would now look to me for spiritual care.

It required me to walk in faith, not just talk about it. It stretched me. It made me depend on Jesus daily. It helped me see that I was no longer called to simply attend church. I was called to serve. I was being called to lead, again. As I reflect on that season, I now realize I was gifted for both the adjunct professor and the recovery chaplain roles. But it was not the season for either. That time would come.

Faith Stays the Course

With time and perspective, it is clear to me now that every moment mattered. Each "yes" I offered to God, even when uncertain and disappointed, became part of a larger story I could not yet see. From the moment I left Guatemala to pursue a second degree, to the quiet mornings I spent praying for clarity in Waco, God was not only guiding me; He was growing me, and He still is.

That is what faith does. It teaches us to listen. It teaches us to remember. It teaches us to keep going.

The Bible is full of people who stayed the course even when things were unclear. Joseph waited in faith. Moses led in faith. Jesus endured in faith. Paul transformed in faith. Samuel discerned in faith. Their lives were not defined by certainty or ease, but by obedience and trust.

They were not perfect, but they were faithful. That is what faith looks like. It walks forward. It stays anchored. It endures.

Faith helps us stay the course, but it does not mean the course will be easy. As we follow Christ, we will face temptation, pressure, and moments of weakness. That is why faith must be joined with purity. Purity is not just about behavior. It is about keeping our hearts clear, our motives surrendered, and our lives aligned with the holiness of God. In the next chapter, we will explore what it means to set an example in purity, not out of fear, but out of love and devotion for the One who calls us.

Scriptures for the Journey

Take time this week to read these verses slowly. Choose one to memorize, meditate on, or write in your journal as a reminder of who God has called you to be.

The righteous shall live by his faith. — Habakkuk 2:4 ESV

So faith comes from hearing, and hearing through the word of Christ. — Romans 10:17 ESV

I have been crucified with Christ and I no longer live, but Christ lives in me. The life I now live in the body, I live by faith in the Son of God, who loved me and gave himself for me. — Galatians 2:20 NIV

Now faith is confidence in what we hope for and assurance about what we do not see. — Hebrews 11:1 NIV

Therefore, since we are surrounded by such a great cloud of witnesses, let us throw off everything that hinders and the sin that so easily entangles. And let us run with perseverance the race marked out for us, fixing our eyes on Jesus, the pioneer and perfecter of faith. — Hebrews 12:1–2 NIV

Pause + Reflect

Take time to pray, journal, or talk through these questions with a trusted friend. You don't have to have all the answers. Just be honest.

1. Where in your life is God asking you to trust Him more deeply?

2. What makes faith feel hard for you right now?

3. What's one step of obedience you could take this week as an act of faith?

Prayer

Father God,

It is in You alone that I place my trust. I confess that apart from You, I can do nothing. You are my source, my strength, my confidence, and my guide. Every good and perfect gift comes from You, and every assignment You've placed before me can only be completed through the power of Your Spirit.

Fill me with unwavering faith, Lord. Not faith in myself, but faith in Your promises, Your power, and Your presence. Help me to walk not by what I see, but by what You have spoken. When I am tempted to shrink back in fear, remind me that You are with me, and that You are faithful to finish what You started. Strengthen me to believe when the way is unclear, to obey when the outcome is uncertain, and to wait with hope when the answer hasn't come.

Anchor me in Your Word, O God. Let Your truth be the foundation I stand on and the light that directs my steps. When doubts whisper loudly, let Your voice be louder. When I hesitate, bring to mind the miracles You've already done and the prayers You've already answered.

Grow my faith, Lord, not just for my sake, but for those watching my life. Let my confidence reflect the faith of Jesus, who trusted You completely, even in suffering. Let my life be a testimony of what is possible when we lean wholly on You.

Make me bold in belief, faithful in action, and consistent in trust. May I be known as one who walks by faith and not by sight.

In Jesus' name,
Amen.

CHAPTER 6

SET AN EXAMPLE IN PURITY

"Blessed are the pure in heart, for they shall see God."
— Matthew 5:8

Purity is not just about what we avoid. It is about what we pursue. It is a posture of the heart that seeks to honor God in motive, thought, and deed. In a world where compromise is common and excuses are expected, choosing to live a life of purity is radical. For a leader, it is necessary.

Paul's charge to Timothy still echoes today: *"Set an example... in purity"* (1 Timothy 4:12 NIV). This kind of example does not begin in public; it starts in private. It is not just about resisting sin. It is about embracing holiness. It is living the same way when no one is watching as you do when everyone is.

Integrity does not begin with behavior, it begins in the mind. Before we talk about motives or actions, we must begin with our thoughts because long before purity is seen, it is shaped in the quiet space of our thinking.

Purity of Thought

Paul tells us to *"take every thought captive to obey Christ"* (2 Corinthians 10:5 ESV). That means purity is not just about actions; it is also about our mental landscape. Our thought life shapes our speech, our choices, and our witness.

Impure thoughts often masquerade as harmless: a judgmental thought about a peer, a lingering fantasy that feeds discontentment, an internal comparison that stirs envy. While others may not see these thoughts, God does and they influence who we become.

King David's fall with Bathsheba did not start with the act of adultery. It started with a glance, followed by a thought, and then a decision. The sin was conceived in the mind before it ever touched his hands. By the time the action came, the battle had already been lost in his thoughts.

Purity of thought requires regular renewal. *"Be transformed by the renewing of your minds"* (Romans 12:2 ESV). This means immersing ourselves in God's Word, not as a checkbox, but as a cleansing. When the Word gets into our minds, it rewires our thinking and aligns us with God's perspective.

When our minds are renewed, our motives begin to shift. We no longer act out of fear, pride, or pressure. We act from a heart aligned with God. Purity is not only about what we think, but why we act.

Purity of Motive

Purity starts with *why* we do what we do. The Pharisees were known for their religious performance, but Jesus called them "whitewashed tombs", meaning they were beautiful on the outside but decaying on the inside (Matthew 23:27). Their actions seemed holy, but their motives were corrupted by pride and self-promotion.

In contrast, Jesus praised the widow who gave two small coins, not because of the amount, but because of her heart. Her motive was pure. Her desire was to honor God. She gave out of love and not for applause.

When our motives are pure, we are not driven by recognition or rewards. We serve because we love. We lead because we are called. We speak because the Spirit compels us. Purity in leadership starts with honest motives, doing the right thing for the right reason, even if no one ever notices.

Purity that begins in thought and flows through motive will ultimately shape our conduct. It shows up in how we carry ourselves, how we treat others, and how we lead under pressure.

Purity of Conduct

Leadership magnifies your life. People watch how you treat others, how you respond to conflict, how you manage pressure. Conduct that is inconsistent with Christ's character discredits your message, no matter how well you preach or teach.

Daniel is one of Scripture's clearest examples of purity in conduct. In Babylon, surrounded by a pagan culture, he stood out not just for his wisdom but for his integrity. When others tried to find grounds to accuse him, they found none, because *"he was trustworthy, and no negligence or corruption was found in him"* (Daniel 6:4).

Daniel's purity was not performative. It was consistent. He prayed daily. He refused to eat defiled food. He honored authority without compromising his faith. As a result, even a pagan king recognized that Daniel's God was worth worshiping.

As modern believers, we are also in a kind of Babylon, surrounded by a culture that normalizes compromise, but like Daniel, our consistent conduct becomes a testimony that points people back to God.

Purity in Relationships

How we treat friends, family, coworkers, or romantic interests reveals the state of our hearts. Purity in relationships is not just about physical boundaries, it is about respect, humility, and mutual honor.

Jesus modeled relational purity in every interaction. He spoke with the woman at the well without crossing lines of impropriety. He corrected Peter without shaming him. He washed Judas' feet knowing he would be betrayed. That kind of love is pure, free from agenda, pride, or manipulation.

Relational purity is about asking, *how can I love this person like Jesus would?* It is about learning to see others as image-bearers of God, not as objects for our benefit or competition for our attention.

Warning Sign: If your relationship consistently requires secrecy, shame, or spiritual compromise, purity is being sacrificed. Love never asks you to sin.

When Leadership Is Hard

Not every leadership moment is a celebratory moment. Some seasons stretch you so deeply that no one would envy your assignment. I walked through one of those hard seasons. I cried driving to work. I cried on the way home. But even in all of that, God called me to stay pure.

God would nudge me to pray, and it was not easy. It felt unfair. I wanted justice. I wanted to be vindicated. Most of all, I wanted to be free, but God would not release me.

So I stayed. I fasted and prayed for months. I read spiritual books during lunch breaks and drove to a park where I would sit and cry and play *"Deliver Us"* from *The Prince of Egypt* on repeat. I kept believing God could change the situation. I kept showing up. But sometimes, it seemed like things only got worse.

One day, it ended. I remember whispering to God, "Thank You." I was so overcome with a sense of relief and what felt like freedom that I went home and took a nap.

Leadership is not always fun. Sometimes it is a fire. The fire will reveal what you carry. I came out of that season refined, not bitter. Not because I had the strength, but because God gave me grace to stay surrendered.

Here is the part I never saw coming. While I was still in that difficult role, God opened the door for me to become an adjunct professor, one of the very things He had once asked me to surrender. Not long after I left, I stepped into a new assignment as a chaplain at an addiction recovery center. Both opportunities had previously been a "no," doors God had once closed. I had released them in obedience, letting go of my plans and trusting His timing.

I forgot about them. He did not. He brought them back not because I pushed for them, but because I surrendered them. Not on my timeline, but in His. Only God.

When No One Sees

The most powerful purity is the kind no one sees. It is the integrity you choose when there is no audience, no affirmation, and no instant reward. In Scripture, we find example after example of quiet obedience that shaped history.

Joseph fled from Potiphar's wife, alone and unseen, Joseph could have given in, but he chose to run, because he feared God more than he desired temporary pleasure (Genesis 39:7–12). His decision cost him in the short term. He was falsely accused and imprisoned (Genesis 39:13–20). But his integrity positioned him for divine promotion.

Then there were the daughters of Zelophehad—Mahlah, Noah, Hoglah, Milcah, and Tirzah. When their father died and left no sons, they stood before Moses and the entire assembly to ask for their inheritance (Numbers 27:1–7). Their request was not born from greed but from righteousness. They sought what was right in God's eyes, not man's. They demonstrated purity of heart by pursuing justice through faith, not manipulation. God Himself affirmed their courage and granted their petition. Their quiet conviction changed the laws of inheritance for generations to come.

Their courage proved that purity is not silence, it is the strength to do what is right in God's sight, even when no one else understands. And nowhere is that purity more fully revealed than in Jesus Himself.

Jesus Himself, the ultimate model of leadership and purity, faced temptation alone in the wilderness. There were no crowds. No disciples. No celebration. Just Him, the enemy, and the wild beasts (Mark 1:13).

He was tempted in every way, just as we are, yet He did not sin (Hebrews 4:15, NIV). His victory in the wilderness affirmed His holiness and pointed to the greater victory to come *becoming the spotless Lamb who would take away the sin of the world* (John 1:29 NIV).

As leaders, we must learn to cultivate purity in the hidden places. What we do when no one is watching reveals who we truly are. God sees the late-night prayers, the private sacrifices, the battles you fight and win in silence, and He honors them.

Hebrews 6:10 reminds us, *"God is not unjust; he will not forget your work and the love you have shown him" (NIV).* Even when no one applauds your choices, heaven does, and heaven's reward is always greater than man's recognition.

Heaven remembers what the world overlooks. Stay faithful. Stay pure. God sees it all.

The Fruit of a Pure Life

Living a life of purity does not mean achieving perfection. It means living with integrity, being honest about your struggles, surrendered in your heart, and consistent in your desire to honor God even when it is hard. Purity is not about having a spotless record; it is about having a submitted spirit.

God does not expect flawlessness, but He does desire faithfulness. A pure heart says, "Lord, I want to please You more than I want to please people or even myself."

Purity produces peace. When your heart is clean, your mind is clear. You do not have to engage in mental gymnastics to cover lies, manage double lives, or pretend to be someone you are not. There is a quiet strength that comes from knowing your private life reflects your public one. You can walk into rooms with your head high and sleep at night without guilt chasing you down.

That is the freedom purity brings. It silences shame and creates space for wholeness. Purity also attracts favor. God honors those who honor Him. Over and over in Scripture, we see that those who choose integrity, even when it costs them something, are met with divine opportunity. Daniel refused to defile himself and was promoted. Joseph resisted temptation and was elevated. Esther kept her character in the palace and saved a nation. Purity positions you for God's best, not just spiritually, but also relationally, emotionally, and vocationally.

Finally, purity amplifies influence. People are drawn to leaders who live what they preach. There is something magnetic about someone who does not just talk about righteousness but embodies it. Jesus said in Matthew 5:8 NIV, *"Blessed are the pure in heart, for they will see God"*. That is not only a promise for eternity. It is a present reality.

The pure in heart perceive God in everyday decisions, in difficult conversations, and in their interactions with others. When your heart is pure, your eyes are clearer, your spirit is lighter, and your influence is deeper. Purity has too often been reduced to teaching abstinence from sex, drugs, and alcohol. While those boundaries matter, they are not the full picture.

If that is all we define as purity in leadership, then we have missed the heart of what it means to follow Jesus. His purity was not defined by avoiding specific behaviors but by His unwavering devotion to the Father and the way He treated people with truth, compassion, and integrity.

Purity is about how we treat others, how we handle influence, and how we live when no one is watching. It means refusing to speak or act with manipulative intent, and honoring people not as a means to an end, but as image-bearers of God to be loved and respected. It means doing good business, keeping your word, and walking in humility. This is the kind of purity that reflects Christ.

Purity is not a punishment. It is a path to peace, clarity, and power. It is not about saying "no" to fun. It is about saying "yes" to freedom. Being an example in purity means living in such a way that others feel safe, inspired, and challenged to pursue God more fully.

Let your life be a mirror, not of culture, but of Christ. May your mind be renewed, your motives refined, and your message redeemed. When others witness a purity that flows from love, not fear, they will not only be drawn to it, they will be transformed by it. You are not just protecting your heart. You are pointing to His.

Scriptures for the Journey

Take time this week to read these verses slowly. Choose one to memorize, meditate on, or write in your journal as a reminder of who God has called you to be.

"Create pure thoughts in me and make me faithful again. Don't chase me away from you or take your Holy Spirit away from me. Make me as happy as you did when you saved me; make me want to obey!" — Psalm 51:10–12 CEV

"Above all else, guard your heart, for everything you do flows from it." — Proverbs 4:23 NIV

"Do you not know that your bodies are temples of the Holy Spirit, who is in you, whom you have received from God? You are not your own; you were bought at a price. Therefore honor God with your bodies." — 1 Corinthians 6:19–20 NIV

"Finally, beloved, whatever is true, whatever is honorable, whatever is just, whatever is pure, whatever is pleasing, whatever is commendable, if there is any excellence and if there is anything worthy of praise, think about these things." — Philippians 4:8 NRSV

"The goal of this command is love, which comes from a pure heart and a good conscience and a sincere faith." — *1 Timothy 1:5 NIV*

Pause + Reflect

Take time to pray, journal, or talk through these questions with a trusted friend. You don't have to have all the answers. Just be honest.

1. How would you describe purity in your own words?

2. What boundaries or habits could you put in place to guard your heart and mind?

3. What's one way you can pursue holiness this week, in thoughts, words, or actions?

Prayer

God,

Help me to walk in purity. In a world full of temptation, strengthen me to resist the enemy and keep my mind stayed on You. Let Your peace guard my thoughts and guide my decisions. You've entrusted me with influence. As I lead, help me to steward that responsibility with integrity, never seeking personal gain but serving others with humility and love. Where sin tries to take root, break every stronghold.

Sever every tie that pulls me away from Your will. Teach me to live by the Spirit and not by the desires of the flesh.

Remind me that everything I have comes from You. Make me generous, not greedy. Help me to see the needs around me and respond with compassion, not self-interest. Where my heart has been wounded, bring healing. Where bitterness hides, uproot it. Keep me tender, teachable, and free from offense.

Let me not strive for perfection on my own, but seek Your holiness through time in Your Word and the joy of my salvation. Purify my mind, my heart, my words, and my actions. Forgive me for the times I have fallen short. Make me holy as You are holy. Fill me afresh with Your Spirit, and let my life reflect You.

In Jesus' name,
Amen.

CONCLUSION

"You are the light of the world. A city built on a hill cannot be hidden."
— Matthew 5:14 NRSV

You do not need a platform or a million followers to lead. What you need is a surrendered heart, a faithful witness, and the courage to follow Christ even when it costs you. The Spirit of God who empowered Timothy is the same Spirit living in you. That means you already carry what you need.

The world is loud, but what it needs is clarity. It needs leaders whose lives align with the truth they profess. It needs people who do not only speak about Jesus but reflect Him in the way they live. It needs leaders rooted in Scripture, guided by love, anchored in faith, and committed to integrity. Leaders who set an example not for attention but because the Gospel demands it.

So where do you go from here? You walk it out. You speak life when it is easier to stay silent. You choose integrity over applause. You love when it is inconvenient. You trust when the path is unclear. You pursue purity when everything around you encourages compromise. You live the example not for recognition, but because Christ lives in you.

Let your life be a message of hope. Let your presence bear the fruit of peace. Let your obedience spark faith in those who feel unseen and unworthy. May those who encounter you come to believe that God can use them too.

If you have made it this far, it is because something within you is stirring, something God placed there long before you picked up this book. That quiet yes in your spirit is the beginning of a bolder life. Not one shaped by fear or perfectionism, but one marked by purpose, obedience, and grace.

You were not only rescued from your past. You have been entrusted with the present. You have been planted in this generation for a reason, and someone's breakthrough may be on the other side of your obedience.

Leadership rooted in consistency is not only about personal purity. It is about giving people something to believe in. When you live out the truth with unwavering integrity, you show others that Jesus is still at work, still calling, and still able to transform lives. Your consistency becomes a beacon of hope in a world that often feels chaotic, where the promises of God may seem distant or delayed. In the face of violence, hatred, and division, you can be the living proof that Christ is still the answer, that faith is still worth it, and that His return is imminent.

Remember, we are not only walking out our faith for ourselves. We are walking it out for the generations to come, those who need a real model of what it means to live for Jesus. It may not always be easy, but the faith we carry will inspire others to keep going. Through every season, trial, and hardship, we must live in a way that encourages believers to remain steadfast, while letting new believers know that God's timing may not always be our own, but He is trustworthy. Lead with love, integrity, and courage. You are not only following a calling. You are helping others see that Jesus is still calling.

And remember this: you do not walk this out alone. The Holy Spirit empowers you to lead with love, purity, and grace. It is the Spirit who gives you strength to persevere when things get tough and courage to stand firm when the world tries to pull you in another direction. Do not rely on your own strength. In Christ, you have been given everything you need.

So lead with endurance. Lead with passion. Lead knowing that every act of obedience and every choice to honor Christ in a broken world is part of a bigger story. It is a story that reaches far beyond your own life and into the lives of others. Your faith, your conduct, and your love are the things that will change the world.

Wherever you are, whether in a warehouse or a boardroom, a classroom or a kitchen, a base overseas or a backyard with your children, you carry the presence of God with you. Your world is not limited to a pulpit or a platform. Your world is the breakroom, the bus stop, the checkout line, the group chat, and the quiet conversations at your kitchen table. And it stretches far beyond borders. Whether you are in Texas or

Tokyo, Guatemala or Queensland, South Africa or South Carolina, this calling is for you. You were not placed there by accident. That space is your mission field, and your life is your ministry. That is where leadership begins, right where you are, with what you have, because God is already with you.

Now you know the charge. You have seen the example. You have counted the cost. It is time to lead, not later and not someday, but now. As you do, may your life be the evidence that Jesus still calls, still equips, and still works through ordinary people to accomplish extraordinary things.

Go lead like it matters, because it does.

Scriptures for the journey

Take time this week to read these verses slowly. Choose one to memorize, meditate on, or write in your journal as a reminder of who God has called you to be.

"Be imitators of me, as I am of Christ." — 1 Corinthians 11:1 ESV

"What you have learned and received and heard and seen in me—practice these things, and the God of peace will be with you." — Philippians 4:9 ESV

"So you received the message with joy from the Holy Spirit in spite of the severe suffering it brought you. In this way, you imitated both us and the Lord. As a result, you have become an example to all the believers in Greece—throughout both

*Macedonia and Achaia. And now the word of the Lord is
ringing out from you to people everywhere, even beyond
Macedonia and Achaia, for wherever we go we find people
telling us about your faith in God." — 1 Thessalonians 1:6–8
NLT*

*"Show yourself in all respects to be a model of good works,
and in your teaching show integrity, dignity, and sound speech
that cannot be condemned, so that an opponent may be put to
shame, having nothing evil to say about us." — Titus 2:7–8
ESV*

*"Don't let anyone look down on you because you are young, but
set an example for the believers in speech, in conduct, in love, in
faith and in purity." — 1 Timothy 4:12 NIV*

Prayer

God,

You are the One who calls, equips, and sends. You do not ask
us to lead from our own strength, but from surrender. You
fill us with Your Spirit and place Your Word in our hearts.
You entrust us with people, moments, and assignments that
reveal who You are.

So here we are, ready and willing. We give You our yes.

Teach us to lead like Jesus. Help us to speak with grace and truth, to walk with integrity and humility, to love without condition, to live by faith and not by sight, to honor You in public and in private, to lead not for applause but out of obedience, and to make You known in all that we do.

When the weight of responsibility feels heavy, remind us that You are our strength. When the path ahead seems unclear, remind us that You are our guide. When we feel disqualified, remind us that You are the One who called us, and You never make mistakes.

Holy Spirit, empower us. Anoint us. Send us.

May our lives be living testimonies of Your glory. May our leadership reflect Your heart, and may every step we take lead others closer to You.

In Jesus' name,
Amen.

SMALL GROUP GUIDE

This guide is designed for small group leaders, friends, or ministries using *Set an Example: How to Lead Others and Live Out God's Presence in the World* together. It is built to support group discussions, personal growth, and Christ-centered leadership development.

Each chapter includes:

- A brief chapter summary
- 4–5 discussion questions (both practical and spiritual)
- A key Scripture
- A closing prayer

Whether you are leading a campus ministry, hosting a book club, or reading with a group of friends, this guide will help you reflect deeply, grow intentionally, and lead faithfully, together.

INTRODUCTION

Summary:

You do not need a position, platform, or title to be a leader. God calls you to influence others through your words, actions, and character.

Discussion Questions:

1. What comes to mind when you hear the word "leader"? Do you see yourself in that picture?

2. Share about a time you influenced someone without even realizing it.

3. How does 1 Timothy 4:12 challenge or support your view of leadership?

4. What is one way this group could lead by example on campus or in the community this week?

Key Scripture: 1 Timothy 4:12

Closing Prayer:

Lord, open our eyes to the ways You've called us to lead. Teach us to influence others with humility and boldness for Your glory. Amen.

CHAPTER 1
DO NOT LET ANYONE LOOK DOWN ON YOU

Summary:

Timothy was young, but Paul reminded him that spiritual maturity, not age, qualifies a leader. This chapter invites readers to overcome doubt, silence insecurity, and trust God's call even when others underestimate them.

Discussion Questions:

1. Have you ever felt overlooked or underestimated in a leadership setting? How did it affect you?

2. What voices—internal or external—tempt you to dim your light?

3. How does Jeremiah 1:6–8 speak to your doubts about being called?

4. What does it mean to lead with confidence rooted in God, not in yourself?

5. How can we support each other in stepping out boldly this week?

Key Scripture: Jeremiah 1:6–8

Closing Prayer:

God, give us courage to lead without fear. Help us silence doubt, trust Your voice, and reflect Your light with boldness. Amen.

CHAPTER 2
SET AN EXAMPLE IN SPEECH

Summary:

Words shape our witness. This chapter explores how godly speech reflects leadership and integrity from everyday conversations to online presence and self-talk.

Discussion Questions:

1. How do you typically use your words? Do they build up or tear down?

2. What challenges do you face in speaking with love and truth?

3. Read James 3:9–10. What is one way to bring more consistency to your speech?

4. How does your online presence reflect your faith?

5. What can our group commit to this week to speak life and encouragement?

Key Scripture: James 3:9–10

Closing Prayer:

Lord, may our words reflect Your heart. Teach us to speak truth with grace and be examples of encouragement, honesty, and love. Amen.

CHAPTER 3
SET AN EXAMPLE IN CONDUCT

Summary:

Your actions preach before you ever say a word. This chapter challenges us to align our lifestyle with our faith, becoming leaders through integrity, service, and consistency.

Discussion Questions:

1. When have your actions spoken louder than your words?

2. Are there areas of your life where your conduct is not aligned with your faith?

3. Who inspires you by the way they live out their beliefs?

4. Read Matthew 5:16. What does it look like for your life to be "light" this week?

5. What is one action you can take this week to reflect Jesus in your everyday life?

Key Scripture: Matthew 5:16

Closing Prayer:

Jesus, help us live in a way that honors You. Let our lives shine with integrity and lead others to Your truth. Amen.

CHAPTER 4
SET AN EXAMPLE IN LOVE

Summary:

Leadership rooted in love mirrors the heart of Christ. This chapter invites us to embody sacrificial, unselfish, Christlike love in a world of self-promotion and superficial care.

Discussion Questions:

1. How do you define love, and how does it compare to the love Jesus modeled?

2. What makes it difficult to love certain people well?

3. Read John 13:34–35. What does "sacrificial love" look like in your relationships?

4. How can we hold each other accountable to love boldly and consistently?

5. What is one way our group can show love to our campus or community this week?

Key Scripture: John 13:34–35

Closing Prayer:

Father, teach us to love as You love with grace, patience, and sacrifice. Let our love lead others to You. Amen.

CHAPTER 5
SET AN EXAMPLE IN FAITH

Summary:

Faith is the anchor of spiritual leadership. This chapter explores how trust in God is cultivated through memory, obedience, and intimacy with the Trinity.

Discussion Questions:

1. What does faith look like in your life right now, in action, not just belief?

2. Share a time when trusting God felt difficult. What helped you stay grounded?

3. Who or what helps you remember God's faithfulness?

4. Read Hebrews 11:6. What step of obedience is God calling you to take in faith?

5. How can our group encourage each other to stay faithful through uncertainty?

Key Scripture: Hebrews 11:6

Closing Prayer:

Lord, deepen our trust in You. Help us remember Your
faithfulness, walk by faith, and stay the course with courage.
Amen.

CHAPTER 6
Set an Example in Purity

Summary:

Purity is more than abstinence, it is the pursuit of holiness in heart, thought, motive, and lifestyle. This chapter reframes purity as a calling, not just a rule.

Discussion Questions:

1. How does the world define purity and how is God's definition different?

2. What does it look like to pursue purity in this season of life?

3. What boundaries, habits, or heart checks help you stay aligned with God?

4. Read Psalm 51:10. How does purity begin with the heart, not just behavior?

5. What steps can we take as a group to support one another in living pure and holy lives?

Key Scripture: Psalm 51:10

Closing Prayer:

Create in us clean hearts, O God. Strengthen our desire for purity, and help us live lives that reflect Your holiness. Amen.

CONCLUSION
SET AN EXAMPLE FOR THE BELIEVERS

Summary:

This final chapter calls young leaders to rise with boldness, rooted in Christlike character. The goal is not perfection but faithful, surrendered leadership that points others to Jesus.

Discussion Questions:

1. Which area: speech, conduct, love, faith, or purity do you feel most challenged to grow in?

2. How has your definition of leadership changed through this book?

3. What fears or doubts are you laying down as you move forward in your calling?

4. Read 1 Timothy 4:12 one more time. What does this verse mean to you now?

5. What is one way you will "set an example" starting this week and who will you lead?

Key Scripture: 1 Timothy 4:12

Closing Prayer:

Lord, thank You for the call to lead. Empower us to be examples in every area of life. May we reflect You boldly, humbly, and consistently. Amen.

NOTES

Use the following pages to write what stood out to you, what you are praying through, and how you sense God leading you to live out what you've learned.

_____

_____

_____

_____

_____

_____

_____

_____

_____

_____

_____

_____

_____

_____

www.ingramcontent.com/pod-product-compliance
Lightning Source LLC
Chambersburg PA
CBHW020739130626
46554CB00006B/2059